Strategic Footsteps

Simple steps to design an effective personal strategy at work

XAVIER J.D. HALBI

Copyright © 2018 Xavier J.D. Halbi

All rights reserved.

ISBN: 1720302340
ISBN-13: 978-1720302346

To our elevation.

CONTENTS

	ACKNOWLEDGEMENTS	vi
	FOREWORD	vii
	INTRODUCTION	x

PART I	STRATEGIC FOOTSTEPS	
1	Goal Setting	Pg #1
2	Where am I?	Pg #25
3	Road map	Pg #48
4	Tools	Pg #54
5	First step	Pg #67
6	Forget	Pg #75
7	Enjoyment	Pg #80

PART II	ESSENTIAL KEYNOTES	
8	Wander	Pg #86
9	Ask around	Pg #90
10	Shit!	Pg #102
11	Crisis	Pg #109
12	Mistakes	Pg #113
13	Steps	Pg #118
14	Change	Pg #125
15	Change your mind	Pg #128

	CONCLUSION	Pg #133
	APPENDIX	Pg #144
	SUGGESTED READING	Pg #172
	REFERENCE LIST	Pg #174

ACKNOWLEDGMENTS

I wish to express all my gratitude to the following:

To Claudia, my wife and spice of my life, thanks to whom I am a person better than I have ever been, and thanks to whom I will become a person better than I am now.

To Aylis, our daughter, who taught me, even before being born, what is important and what is not so important.

To Everyone who crossed my path, physically or virtually for each has been a teacher.

FOREWORD

I have read more than 100 business books a year every year since 1989, and I can count on one hand, with a few fingers left over, the number of books I've read that deliver as much true business and life wisdom as this one does. Regardless of where you are in your career, on the following pages you will learn valuable lessons that will help you avoid painful mistakes, make better decisions, suffer less stress, reduce negative conflict, vastly improve your communication skills, become a more effective leader, build a stronger business and create a happy and successful life. That is a big promise, but it is true.

Achieving success in business and life does not happen from chance, fate or good luck, it comes from creating and implementing a set of focused strategic steps that consistently move you in the direction of your vision. In this book, Xavier has compiled some of the best advice and guidance from leading thinkers throughout time, and gives you specific tools, examples and workshops to help you apply those powerful ideas. What you'll learn in this book can be life-changing, but it won't be easy. It will require focus, hard work and sacrifice. And if you want to be successful, the truth is you have no choice. Let me tell you why…

For more than 15 years, I have been teaching an executive level strategy program as a guest lecturer at the Wharton School of Business, and I begin every session with this the equation:
II>EI

Here is what it means, "For your business to be successful in the future, the rate of Internal Innovation must exceed the rate of External Innovation." In other words, to win in the marketplace your organization must innovate, create, strategize and execute better than any of your competition. Your company must be smarter, faster, more agile and adaptable than any other organization in your space. That is an extremely difficult challenge, but even more challenging is the fact that for YOU to be successful in the future you must innovate, create, learn, adapt, change and execute faster than anyone else in the world who does what you do. Think about that for a second, it should scare you, I know it scares me. This is an incredibly daunting challenge, however, there is a term used in this book: *Jichigakuzen* (you will have to read the entire book to find out what it means) that I believe will give you the answer of how to accomplish this successfully.

Several years ago I was asked to give a TED talk about the most important thing I've ever learned in my life and I would like to share that with you. After failing out of college on the first try, I graduated in the top four the United States in my major on my second try and was named CEO of an international company at the age of just 26. How did I make that turn around? Two key ideas:

Ask for help. This is the second most important thing I've ever learned in my life. Most people think that asking for help shows weakness, but the most successful people I have ever worked with, which includes several billionaires, were superb at asking for help, input, feedback and advice.

Which leads me directly to the most important thing I've ever learned: You become what you focus on, and like the people you surround yourself with. Whatever you fill your mind with and whoever you choose to spend your time with, will directly determine what your life will look like a decade from now.

One of the ways to do that is to by spending time with bright, sharp, smart and talented people and… asking them for help. Another great way to is to read books like this one. Xavier has taken the time to put together all the best things he's ever learned in this book for you. He will help you overcome obstacles, avoid missteps, take advantage of opportunities, grow, excel and create a wonderfully successful business career and life. And it isn't just some theory, he has learned this through personal experience. I've had the great honor to serve as a mentor to Xavier and have watched him apply the ideas in this book to make dramatic positive changes in his life. And I also know that this book was born from his deep passion to share these ideas and help other people achieve success too.

So, take what you learn in this book seriously, be thoughtful, be disciplined and apply your new-found knowledge with vigor and determination. Change is possible, success is achievable, many of the answers you are looking for are just a chapter or two away. Enjoy!

I wish you every possible happiness and success.
John Spence, February, 2018
Author of "Awesomely Simple",
Top 100 Business Thought Leader in the America,
Top 500 Leadership Development Expert in the World

INTRODUCTION

Strategy is a big word that has been used in all sorts of ways. It means so much, and at the same time doesn't mean much anymore. Strategy, simply put, is: knowing where you're going and having an action plan to get there. In this book I intend to bring about a clear step-by-step process to devise a strategy that can be applied easily. Also, you will have some techniques, mnemonic points to assist you in the designing of your strategy, questions to answer which will define your goals, and guide you on the road to success. This book is specifically targeted to your business life, whether it is your career, your business decisions about your team, your department or even your company.

Why I wrote this book.

Throughout my career, I have seen an exponential increase of jargonization applied at work and a thought/belief that pushes people to make things complicated to look smarter or even pretend to be an expert. Two books were really the triggers for me;
Simplicity – Edward DeBono which really made me realize how much people, our society to some extent, tend to complicate things.

Awesomely Simple – John Spence . John is not only a mentor to me, he is also an inspiration. In his very down to earth approach, he literally put business into a simple formula, easy to replicate and that drives results. I have myself applied this formula to several areas in my career and to the many departments I have worked in, and it works!

In my line of work, I have been working designing strategies for the business for many years, in several different areas of the hospitality industry; from serving clients, to booking processes, to price positioning, marketing, to sales, from managing systems to managing people, to coaching them, to leading them. Strategy is a word that is used in absolutely every area of the business life... to no end.

Throughout the hundreds of hours spent training my colleagues on how to take a strategic approach to business, it became clear to me that we really want to make the "beast" look a lot more scary and mysterious than it actually is. Honestly, we are not trying to build a rocket to send people on Pluto! However, the thinking process to even achieve that "feat" is not complicated. Even the thinking process to even achieve that feat is not complicated. It is complex however, for it comprises a very large amount of details and pieces, like the numerous intricate simple threads that make a tapestry look overwhelmingly detailed and grandiose. Each in itself is quite simple, but put together in number, the entire oeuvre becomes complex and beautiful.

So my aim really is to debunk the myth that strategy is complicated. Through this book, I made a point to keep the language easy, approachable and simple to read and the principals detailed are easy to apply.

I have read hundreds of business books, watched hundreds of videos on management and leadership, I have attended many trainings and seminars, I have gone through a Cornell MBA to learn more about business... All the talk is about how to increase market share, market value, how to capture an increasingly high number of customers, marketing to a larger audience, to the right audience, how to make your employees more motivated, how to make them work more effectively, how to sell your product and services more effectively, how to make the business more cost efficient, more profitable. And you know what is missing in my opinion? Talking to the people as the workforce, the people who are doing the job themselves, the people who serve the customers, the individuals who make the company, to talk to them directly and help them be more confident at work, more efficient, to give them the understanding of what is going on in people's heads, the knowledge of why people behave the way they do, why they react the way they do, so that they need to survive and thrive in the corporate world, for them to be more strategic with their own lives. Why "at work"? Because out of our 24 hour days, we spend at least 9 hours there, even more if you work in the Hospitality industry like me, then you average 60 hours a week during your entire career. Let's keep 9 hours in mind, then add about 8 hours of sleep (if you make sure that you do not compromise on this) 2 hours of transportation per day, 1 hour for getting ready in the morning, breakfast… What we are left with is around 4 hours in our day to do something else than work. I heard recently a cool speech: We work 40 years of our lives, to get 40% of our salaries (the rest goes to the governmental taxes, VAT…) and when we retire, we get only 40% of this money. We spend so much time at work that it has become like the main reason for us to be here on earth! We literally live to work.

Over 20 years of experience, I have started at the bottom of the ladder, like you, I have started out by carrying luggage of clients who thought that simply because they had the money, they owned me… and they certainly did, because when they asked for me to fetch something outside of the hotel, I was very excited and happy to do so because I liked to be the go-to guy, but I also hoped to get a juicy tip. Needless to say that I did not always receive what I expected for the run. I worked in housekeeping to clean the toilets of clients whom I was serving afterwards at lunch (after washing and disinfecting my hands, I promise) guests who would put the rest of their food on the floor because someone is paid to clean after them, I served customers who would whistle and snap their fingers to call the waiters, guests screaming at the reception because something was not of their liking, or because they wanted to get something for free, or simply because they had a bad day. All the time, the customers always wanting more and the supervisor always wanting more too. In the service industry, aren't we all victims of the dilemma that is very common: *"the customer is always right"* and *"my boss is the one who pays me to do the job"*? Like most people working in an organization, I have gone through the difficult times of not knowing what my boss wanted from me, of expecting the worst of the next meeting, taking comments very personal because I was just passionate about my work, everything became a personal complaint towards me. Some colleagues have been selfish, some have been playing politics while I was stubborn enough not to play the game myself, some have spread false rumors and some betrayed me, some have cut the grass under my feet so that I could look weaker and they could shine more. I have been a curious employee extra motivated, I have gone through the difficult times of self-doubt, wondering if I was good enough, if I was in the right industry, I also felt deeply the stress of low self-esteem and low confidence. I have been a rising star, a very thought-after specialist in the entire Middle East region, I have felt the weight of people's envy and jealousy. I have gone through the uncertainty of knowing if today was the last one in this company, to the depression that intense political games eventually bring to anyone who stays in it for too long. Like most people I had the pressure of being the one to bring the bread and butter home, to getting even more responsibility as "the man of the family" when my wife Claudia announced that she was pregnant of our daughter. Although this blessed moment was a turning point that made me say "*I will not bring this stress back home to my wife and child*", I unfortunately fell right into it a couple of years later. Like so many people, I tried to prove myself to my boss, to my father even, to my colleagues, trying to justify my reason to be here, to prove myself to my wife as well, and deep down, to myself. So much of our day, so much of our lives is spent at work, going through this emotional roller-coaster. And for some reason, companies believe that employees are paid for this, so we should not complain. A manager is responsible for the results of his department and of his team, he is responsible for the team effectiveness, he is responsible for the company's performance, so it should be the responsibility of our managers to ensure that we are treated in the most efficient way so that our productivity is optimized, right? Unfortunately it is rarely the case. Let's be honest, if you do not take care of your own health & career, who will? So take charge; take your career, your progression, your goals and your life in your own hands.

We have all gone through this. How much I wished I had more clarity about what was going on! I did not have a clear picture of what I wanted, I did not have the understanding of why people are the way they are, including myself, I did not have the insights of what I should expect from others and I did not have the tools to face them.

Well I wrote this book because my life would have been very different if I had received these earlier, and my life has dramatically changed since I have them. In this book I wanted to share with you the insights that I have collected, share with you what I have noticed, analyzed and realized through all these years of experience in the trenches. The knowledge and insights that I have gained, experimented with and worked with, the tools that have helped me and that I still use to date, and that you yourself can apply and benefit from in the work environment are here in this book. It will help you clear the path for your journey to become an enjoyable and successful one. This book is not for your company which will still be here after you retire, this book is for you.

What can you expect to find in this book?

In this book, I break down my strategic thinking into a very simple 7-step approach that can be applied in any area of work immediately. You will find examples of my own experience, as well as tips, hints, suggestions for you to use straight away.

Part I of the book details what the 7 steps are. These 7 steps are very similar to what you go through when preparing for a trek in nature. This metaphor makes sense to me, not only because I feel very close to nature and love to walk in the wilderness, but because your career, your job is a journey in itself.

Part II will bring your attention to sign posts that are highly important to keep in mind in order to make the 7-step approach work even better in your favor. This is the ointment that makes the machine run smoother.

These simple steps are as follows:
1. Goal setting
2. Where am I?
3. Road map
4. Tools
5. First step
6. Forget
7. Enjoyment

It is a gradual process, hence the title Strategic

footsteps and it is also about paying attention to what is right under our noses every day of our lives, and that we unfortunately do not always see.

Because the aim of this book is to equip you with an effective framework for successful strategy implementation, it is not a material to scheme through in an afternoon. You will get as much from this book as you put in thinking things through for yourself as you go along. It happens many times that situations appear to be as overwhelming as a mountain. You have a goal to reach the top of that mountain, but that goals seems far, if you are able to see more than one path, you will feel confused, and some of them look long, some appear to lead nowhere, and some look dangerous even. But we are here to embarking on a journey together. Step by step we will reach that summit.

We will especially spend ample time in the "tools" section. The vast majority of accidents in the wilderness are caused by either a lack of knowledge, skills or preparation (training). All these are collected and gathered under this section. "Tools" are unfortunately the one key ingredient that most companies lack to provide their employees with. I like to look at situations in the following simplifying way: Either there is a system issue or a person issue. If there is a problem with the system then we need to fix it so that our employees can do their job properly. If it is a person issue, then 2 options: Is it an attitude issue or is it a skills issue? If it is an attitude issue, then we have probably not hired the right person for the job in the first place. However, I also believe that we have the right people in the wrong place. This means that we have to do with who we have on board; in my books, nobody is getting fired just for not being the right fit. It also means that I have the belief that although this person is not in the right place here, s/he will be the right fit somewhere else, in another team, in another department… If the issue comes from a lack of skills, then we have a training issue.

Training is a core discipline in a company. Some companies do not offer enough training to their staff, but most companies deliver training that is only scratching the surface of the job requirement; they teach only the bare minimum for you to do the job. Most of the time, the trainings that are very motivating, giving the skills to work as a team... is offered only to the higher management in the company. Whether at school, or in the form of training, classroom or online, development of skills, the tools that you can have at your disposal to make you more efficient, to get things done, to improve yourself and your teams are rarely available to the staff. In this book, you will learn the ones that will consolidate the foundations of your growth.

You will also take a path of personal discovery through some tests (not to worry, there is no-one to judge you; there is no best answer anyway). The results will help you find out the key points for you to focus on and that will catapult your performance in many areas such as communication, clear goal setting, understanding your strengths, your values, realizing what makes you tick, and what to do with that, getting to know what works best for you,... and many more insights.

I strongly encourage you to take the time to do the exercises, to be honest and open with yourself, as well as to fill in your results and grids. They will bring a new light and understanding of yourself, of your team members and your company. This will also point out the areas that you can focus on to improve your performance as well as that of your teams. Of course, as a bonus, these steps will guide you in the formulation of your strategy, from the drawing board to its implementation.

Unfortunately, this is the kind of things that no one teaches you, neither at school, nor in high school, not even in an MBA. But don't be afraid, it is not complicated at all, and we will go at your own pace. Take it easy.

I genuinely believe that if everyone were to take something from this 7-step formula and had the tools that you will discover for yourself, there would be more business people living a more peaceful life, more fruitful, that they would be more inspiring to their teams and colleagues, and that the business would be even more profitable and more enjoyable than ever... because everything starts with the employee, everything starts with you.

Enjoy the ride.

STRATEGIC FOOTSTEPS

Part I

STRATEGIC FOOTSTEPS

CHAPTER 1.

GOAL SETTING.

KNOW YOUR GOAL, MAKE IT CLEAR, CONCISE AND SMART

Let's get started! Let's imagine you want to embark on a long march to reach the top of a mountain. From down here, the mountain looks impressive and you cannot even see the top from here. You can however imagine the summit. Now, even then the goal will not be clear and so it is very easy to get lost on the way to the top.

Goal setting is an essential skill to possess, even more so in a work environment. Not only for one's performance, but also for one's own career. Indeed, you may expect or even hope that your supervisor or manager plans your career advancement and for him to make all the arrangements for your next step, but in reality, it rarely happens. So the real and more important question is: *what do you do about it?* Are you reactive, waiting for people to come at your doorstep and ask, if not beg you to come work for them, running the risk of being placed (by your boss) in a job that serves him and not necessarily you? Or do you want to take charge of your fate? Are you passively waiting for your performance to show and hopefully and patiently wait for someone to notice you are in the room or do you manage your life and proactively pursue your endeavors?

There are two kinds of direction that people organize their goals into; there are people who are "Avoiders" and people who are "Wanters". No style is better than the other, it is just the way people sort out their focus.

Those "avoiders" avoid issues, challenges, difficulties. This of course can be very useful at times; imagine a person who is not "avoiding" and therefore drives carelessly, they do not put the seatbelt on, they are the phone while driving, they just change lanes as they go without looking around,… these people are reckless. Avoiders, unfortunately face difficulties when they set goals or when they try to get things moving because of they give too much attention to potential issues and challenges they think will come.

On the other hand, a "Wanter" is someone who sets their minds to what they want, they go forward towards what they desire to achieve, possess, attain… These people focus on the goal that they set. This is an attitude that is very useful to get things done. They are action-oriented and they "go for it". Unfortunately, this orientation can also be double-edged because this person is very likely to disregard, ignore, or even be totally oblivious to the challenges ahead.

Practically, a person might have goals that sound like this: *"to stop having stress"*, *"stop getting crap from my boss"*, *"not to have incapable employees"*, *"to stop losing money"*, *"not to receive complaints from my clients"*… All these goals are fine, but they are not as compelling and attractive as if they were stated in a positive form; *"I want to have happy customers"*, *"I want my company to be profitable"*, *"I want my colleagues to respect me"*, *"I want my boss to recognize my worth"*, *"I want to collect funds for my organization*", "*I want to be promoted*"... These are examples of goals, statements that are formulated in the positive. They suddenly become more attractive, more interesting to go forward to reach them, and therefore they seem more concrete. You can automatically feel the drag of the negative statements as you read them, and you feel the upbeat and energy in those that are positively formed.

Going back to getting set for our trek on that mountain; there is a very big difference between telling yourself: "*I don't want to face challenges on my way, I don't want to get hurt, I don't want to get lost on the way*" and "*I want to reach the summit of this mountain, I want to conquer this beast, I want to feel what it is like to be at the top, looking at what I have achieved*". Big difference, isn't it?

A relatively "good" or a more preferable direction is therefore one that encompasses both aspects "wanter" and "avoider", without being at one extreme or the other, and one that is formulated in the positive; "*I want my boss to recognize my contribution to the team* (we will get back to this specific portion in a bit), *and I am also aware of the challenges I will have to have this executed...*"

An effective goal has to be real, achievable and motivating so much so that you feel seduced by it, compelled to go towards it, work for it, that you feel pulled forwards as if you had not much choice.

Most of us have heard about **SMART** goals. If you have not, here is a detailed explanation. If you are very familiar with this, jump to the section "A smarter goal?".

SMART stands for:
- Specific
- Measurable
- Accountable
- Relevant
- Trackable

Specific

A goal that is vague has no power and it will hardly motivate anyone but a dreamer, certainly not an achiever. The goal has to be specific enough that it has a shape and becomes material, almost palpable. Too vague and it loses power, too specific and it loses the fluidity and the room for flexibility. Imagine yourself at the bottom of the mountain and telling yourself *"I want to get there* (the top)" that does not sound very interesting. One could say: *"Well this mountain is far, how about you go up this hill instead?"* However, if you say: *"I want to climb this specific mountain* (and not another, for whatever reason you may have)", *"I want to see the scenery for myself from that mountain top* (because the photos you have seen from there look amazing)", *"I want to be at the top of Mount Everest"*, then this is much more specific.

If one says: *"I want to be rich"* this is too vague to know what kind of riches we are referring to; material, financial, spiritual, knowledge, emotional riches,... are we talking about abundance, opulence, dilettantism,... ? But if one says *"I want to be a millionaire"* then the goal is a little bit more specific. We know now that it is a financial goal and that the amount is equal or above 1 million. We have yet to know if this amount is in monetary terms or in Assets, and what currency we are talking about (1 million Indian Rupees is far from being US$ 1 million).

In the Disney movie *Aladdin*, the hero of the story, Aladdin, tells the genie from the bottle that he wishes to be "a prince". *"Your wish is my command"* said the genie... and the only thing that Aladdin got was a new set of clothes, an elephant and several people and animals around him... hardly any kingdom, money or anything else that would have lasted longer than the parade did (they all disappeared at the end of it).

"I want to be promoted" ... your wish is my command ... pouf! And you have the title of the level above, but in

another department (not really the one you were expecting or hoping for).

"*I want to have a higher salary*"… your wish is my command … pouf! And on Jan 1st, you have a 1% increase in your salary while the inflation is of 4%.

Be Specific with your goals.

Once you got that straight, then your goal needs to be measurable.

Measurable

You cannot control and manage what you cannot measure. A very simple way to make a goal measurable is to answer the question: "*How will I know when I have achieved it?*" If your answer is not sharp with a sense of certainty to it, if it does not have a quantifiable measure, then the goal will be very likely slipping through your fingers time and time again. Will you know that you have reached the top of the mountain because you will take a picture from there that is similar to the one you have seen on internet? Do you wish to reach the summit today? This year? One day?

Going back to the idea of being rich; being "rich" is not a measure. Once you reach US$10,000 in your bank account, you might tell yourself; "*Wow that was not that bad, I want more, I can do more, I'll work a bit more*", then you reach US$100,000. After which you tell yourself; "*Oh come on, just a bit more*"… to no end.

However, when you set a target, then you know that you have achieved it because of the threshold, of the measure you have set for yourself. The question "*Have I achieved my goal?*" will have only 2 possible answers: "yes" or "no". Having such a kind of threshold makes your achievement very clear; you achieve or you do not, it's black or white… and until you have, you haven't.

A colleague of mine was telling me about retiring when he has enough money. So I asked him, how much is "enough"? … To which he had no answer. It then dawn to him that enough was never enough, and as I saw the bulb lite above his head almost instantaneously, I asked him to put a number on "enough". Then a deadline.

The goal *"I want to manage people"* is specific, but not measurable (enough). Yes you will know when you manage people in your company when you will have at least one associate under you. But is this what you meant? How many employees do you want to manage for you to know that you are managing people? 5, 50, 100? More? How many?

That is specific, and measurable.

Accountable / Actionable

Many people say that "A" in SMART stands for Achievable. But if the goal is to be Realistic ("R") then it is Achievable. So in order to make it less redundant, more practical and a lot more empowering, I prefer to make the goal Accountable. After all, this is your goal – or the goal of the person you are giving it to – not anyone else's, right? So own it!

The "A" also stands for Actionable. Imagine having a goal that would require you to do nothing about it… what kind of goal would that be? You would be standing at the foot of the mountain and "wish" you could be at the top. *"Well, what do you do about it, then? Sit there and wait for the mountain top to come to you?"*

So the idea about the goal to be actionable is for you to take things in your own hands; let's go back to the sentence: *"I want my boss to recognize my contribution to the team"*. There is "I", which is a good step, however the action is taken by someone else (your boss who does the "recognition" of your contribution). You really want to take ownership of your goal by owning the action that need to take place. Empower yourself so that you become the "actioner". How different and more powerful does this sound instead: *"I want to find a way to make my boss acknowledge my contribution to the team"*? how about: *"I want to be able to convince my boss of my…"*? and how about this one: *"I want to find the resources that I need to demonstrate to my boss the contribution I bring to the team"*? Play with this a little bit and make your own sentences. Just remember that you are the one to take action and that your boss and the team are not "actioners" in your goal.

Now you can give a goal to an associate, to your team, or to yourself to reach, but you need to make someone accountable to reach it. It is not about blaming if the goal is not reached, it is about knowing the points of contact to be used in order to make sure that the team or the person, or yourself are on target. And of course, the recognition that goes with it if the target is reached.

In addition, and as a bonus, to make a goal Accountable & Actionable promotes ownership and responsibility to the person "in charge" so that motivation follows as it naturally emerges from that individual or team. There is then a sense of purpose, and hopefully striving for achievement. So, for your goal to be "Promoted Team Leader in your department", you will not only count on your boss to do that for you (he has the power to make it happen) but you will not wait for him to read your mind and see through his crystal-ball that you want a promotion. You will take the responsibility to talk to your boss about what you would like; you will ask him what you need to do for this to happen, what are the conditions for you to have it, what targets you need to reach, what you need to improve, and how this can be measured and when. And all this is your responsibility and yours alone.

Remember that you cannot control or manage what you cannot measure. How many times have you been judged or you have heard employees being rated or judged with no actual measure?

Now you might have seen some bosses proactively approach their employees and talk to them about their future, their wishes, endeavors, their hopes, dream,… but let's be Realistic – it is also the "R" in these goal-setting criteria – this is a cherry on the cake, and it is not as commonly experienced as one would hope in the work place.

Relevant / Realistic / Reachable

A goal that is set to be unrealistic defeats the purpose of setting a target. What is the point of aiming at the target if we know that the arrow will not reach it because it is too far? Too many managers set unrealistic targets to "stress" or push the team, which inevitably turns into demotivation, lack of passion, drop in energy, drop in excitement, and it will invariably transform into low performance (aka: below target... duh!).

Would it be realistic to climb this mountain without prior training, knowledge of the landscape without having done any mountain climbing before or without tools with you, without a tent, without food and water even?

A goal has the purpose of being reachable, or to give a sense of attainability. Most Olympic athletes give themselves a target that is few centimeters further or higher that their record, because these are attainable, but even if they fall short of that target by few centimeters, they do break their personal past performances and thereby grow. And this motivates them to do even better the next time.

Your goal also needs to be Relevant. Is your goal aligned with what really matters? Is your goal in line with a higher purpose, a bigger picture, something bigger than you? Is it serving a larger system? Is your goal tackling the issue that is at hand or is it side tracking you and your team? Let's imagine that the sales of your company have been taking a dive for the past few weeks or months, and you set the goal to have all the administrative work automated, with the appropriate specificity and measures that we addressed already. Is this goal relevant to this situation? Is this goal tackling the root of the problem for the drop in sales? Is achieving this goal going to make the needle move in anyway… in the timeframe that is hopefully short enough to impact the business faster rather than later? The relevance of the goal is highly important if you wish to have a laser sharp focus and most efficient way to reaching it.

A great way to find this out is by simply asking yourself the question *"Why?"* 3 times: *"Why do you want to reach this goal?"* Once you have an answer, again ask yourself: *"Why?"* And once you have an answer to that question, ask again: *"Why?"* By then you will have a pretty good idea if you are tackling the right issue.

Trackable / Time

Setting a time limit to a goal gives yet another dimension to the target. When do you want to reach the top of this mountain? One day? Today? In a year from now? To tell yourself that you want to be promoted to the next level in your current department is one thing, but it might take more time than you had anticipated. This might lead to impatience, frustration, even jealousy, a rise in sarcasm and anger towards your boss and/or colleagues and eventually it will work against you and your promotion.

However, if you say: *"I want to be promoted to team leader in this department within the next 2 months* (if this timeframe is realistic)", this gives a perspective that will allow you to concentrate on your job and on what is necessary to achieve that goal, in that time frame. Tracking your progress or that of your employee (to whom you gave a SMART goal) is as important as the time frame. Indeed, it is crucial to know if you are on track to achieving your goal.

When I have a new report joining my team, I like to probe and ask questions to understand better how I need to interact with that person in order to have a more effective communication and draw out the most of our new relationship for the benefits of all parties. One of these questions that I find paramount to ask them is: *"When I will give an assignment or a project, should I let you be until the deadline is reached or should I check in on you from time to time, and if so, how often?"*. At first, the person might tell you that it is fine to let her be, but by digging further you will get the true need answer that will be most effective.

I find this very import to ask for what works best for you. Have you ever had a boss who was giving you too much freedom when you needed to be followed up upon – maybe because the project did not get your buy-in or you were not motivated about it? Or did you have a boss who followed up on you so much that you felt like he was doubting your capacities and lacked trust in you?

What tracking system and how often works best for you, or for your team, to reach your goal? Go find out; I guarantee you, you might be surprised by the answers, but even more so by this effectiveness of knowing that beforehand.

PS: even your deadline must be Realistic.

Few tip-questions
So ask yourself, now:
-What long-lasting goal have you not been able reach, yet?

-Do you need time to (re-)formulate it, or does it come out of your head straight away?

-How vague or specific is that goal?

-How much clarity do you have about it?

-Is it a negatively or positively phrased goal?

A smarter goal?
You will automatically and straight away notice that once you have set a goal to be SMART the feeling is quite different; it looks more concrete, almost palpable, and more

attainable. Now that we are on the same page with those who had heard of SMART goals before, I would like to introduce to you a way to make your goal even **SMARTER**. That is by simply adding 2 more components to it:
- Environment
- Resources

Environment

This refers to the environment in which you live in, the people around you, those who will be affected directly or indirectly by your attaining your goal, but also yourself. This point answers the question: *"Once you reach this goal, how will that change you, your life and the way you are now* (before reaching the goal)".

Climbing a mountain, whether rock climbing or trekking can be quite a feat. This requires to push our own limits, some level of personal commitments, some blood and sweat that as an overall experience can change someone's life. Several years ago, my Claudia and I have taken to do a trek in the Annapurna (Nepal). We had no or little preparation for this and with our Sherpa friends we walked through the mountain range, up and down several thousands of stairs. All in all it took us 12 hours per day for 7 days to walk a distance that others were doing in 10 days. We rode on a bus that was for 5 hours literally on the verge of falling in a 300m precipice, we ran away from Maoists who wanted to rob the group of tourists lodging in the same inn, Claudia discovered during the trip that she had rheumatoid arthritis, we met very interesting people, we shared bread with strangers, we slept in stone cold places, we washed in ice-cold water. It was dangerous, tiring, painful, but gosh was it worth it! We did it, and the experience changed both of us.

Back to work and to your life. Say you want to be

making $10,000 a month from other sources of income than your current job, in one year time from now. An environment question would be: *"Who else is going to be affected by this goal?; during the entire process of walking towards that goal as well as when I eventually reach that goal?"*

Well, maybe you will have to leave earlier from work to make sure that you have the time to do the research on how to do that, do your things after working hours because some offices close at the same time as you finish work. How will you be affected during your working hours? Will you be daydreaming?, which might affect your performance in your current job? Or do you need to work more and longer hours? How will this process and period affect your family, friends and social life?

Once you achieve your goal, and make these $10,000 a month, then what? Will you quit your job? How is this going to affect your relationship with your family, parents, siblings, your friends…?

All these questions are essential to ask yourself because your achieving your goals will not only affect you; it will have ripple effects that will impact larger systems around you.

Resources

These are the tools that are needed in order for you to achieve your goal. Resources can be material (tools, hardware, physical things, vehicle…) financial, or even immaterial (spirit, a certain attitude, motivation, self-confidence, self-esteem, skills…).

If you go trekking, you definitely want to know what kind of terrain you are going to walk through, because you will need different tools and utensils accordingly: forest, jungle, water, rocky land, desert, snow, ice… Imagine you have a heating blanket with you when you go to cross the desert. Not very useful is it? Or you have no way of heating yourself up when the land you are going to walk through is very damp. Not very convenient.

Knowing in advance what is necessary for you to perform and achieve the goal set is a key point on this check list. For instance, to want to be promoted to the next level might require the acquisition of certain skills such as managerial, analytical, communication, social, coaching, computer skills, budgeting skills, people/soft skills... that you might not possess... yet. But once you have identified which resources you need, you will be even more apt to go and get them for yourself... and guess what? This is also part of Accountability given from you to yourself.

And how about having the smartest goal of all?
How do you feel about your goal now? It is clearer, isn't it?

That is because you have a SMARTER goal... but let's work on you having the **SMARTEST** one, shall we?
- Sensory
- Touching/Taking you whole

Senses/Sensory
When learning about goal-setting, you might have heard of the term "Visualize your goal". The idea is to project & see in your mind's eye the goal as if you had achieved it already. What I suggest here is to take it further by imagining what you will see once your goal is achieved.

Most high level athletes do this practice before the exercise; a skier closes his eyes and visualizes the full slalom parkour before launching himself on the ski slope, an F1 driver does the same about the entire circuit, visualizing every single curve of the road, a sprinter will see himself run the race and cross finish line...

Imagine being in the situation, in the midst of it, already; imagine you are inside the picture, and make it a movie. You have full control of what you imagine, for imagination is one of our most powerful capabilities. Bring some adjustments so that the colors of what you perceive are vivid, bright and the image is as clear as possible. Notice as much detail as you can. Take your time.

Now notice the sounds that you can perceive in the situation where your goal is achieved. Imagine what the people involved will tell you. Do you recognize the voices of some people you know? Some people who were supporting you all along maybe, or someone who did not believe in you but is bound to face the fact that "you did it"? What tone of voice will they use? What key words are they using? How does that make you feel? Maybe your own voice? What will you tell yourself once your goal is achieved? What is the word, expression, exclamation that you will tell yourself and that will let you know that "you did it"?

You might even feel objects or people around you. It could be the touch of a congratulating hand, a pat on the back, an object symbolizing your successfully achieving your goal, money,... anything. Move your hands around, act as you will act when you have achieved your goal, feel with your hands what you feel.

Touching / Taking you whole

Once you successfully went through the previous point of making your goal as sensory clear as possible, you will feel something inside. Now, whether it is a sense of peace, satisfaction, accomplishment, happiness, joy, excitement, euphoria... You now become aware of a shift inside of you that let you know for certain that your goal is achieved. You may notice the location of that feeling somewhere, and then the shape of it, the color or colors that it has, maybe a sound as well.

You may also notice a movement of the feeling. Let this feeling spin around, faster, and faster, and it grows, and grows, and grows so much that your entire body is eventually bathed inside of that feeling... until this very pleasant and positive feeling takes you whole. You might feel other sensations as well, a change in temperature, a tingling sensation, light headed, or even your body is lighter. Stay with it for a while and enjoy this moment. It is yours.

Here is below a recap of each step to formulating an effective and powerful goal setting strategy. You can use this for any goal that you have for yourself or for your team.

Each point is described with a typical question you should be able to answer for yourself. On the right-hand side, you have some free space to jot down your points.

Is your goal SMATER and is it even the SMARTEST one?

Criteria *Sample questions to answer*	**Description** of the goal by section
S – Specific *What do I really <u>want</u> to achieve?* *(stated in the positive)* *What are the specifics and rough details of this goal?*	
M – Measurable *How will I know when I have reached my goal?* *What will let me know that "this is it"?*	
A – Accountable *Do I believe that this is up to me to make it happen?* *Do I own it?* *Do I make my team responsible for achieving it? (for a goal imposed on someone else)*	

R – Relevant/Realistic *Is it aligned with your outcome?* *Is this goal realistically achievable, even if it means putting a lot of efforts, energy or attention to it?*	
T – Trackable *What is my deadline to reach this goal?* *What is the timeline of the milestones I give myself to reach this goal?*	
E – Environment *What might happen when the goal is reached?* *Who else will be affected during the process <u>and</u> once it is achieved?*	
R – Resources *Do I have the tools, material, skills or knowledge to achieve this goal?* *Does the team/person have the tools, power or means to reach this goal?*	
S – Synaesthesia/ Senses/Sensory *Describe what you see, what you hear, what you smell, with as much detail as you can, of the entire situation & surrounding*	

T – Touch *Describe how you feel inside, now that you have achieved this goal. Where is the feeling? What shape, color, sound?*	

Make this goal yours!

In addition to helping people achieve their goals through the above acronym, I also like to teach my audience that a goal should be **MINE**. It might sound like it is close to Accountability, but it goes a lot deeper than that; MINE stands for:
- My goal
- Inspired / Insight / Intuition
- New
- Excitement, Energized

My goal

Many caretakers push their dependents to do what they would have loved to do, what they believe is better for them. Bosses or so-called mentors tell their trusted mentees what they should do, what path they should follow, because they have followed the same path years ago, generations ago, where and when the corporate world, the market conditions, the technology, the world were completely different.

The book *The magic of thinking big* – David Schwartz is inspiring and will fill you up with a renewed energy to reach out for your own goals and dreams. It will inspire you to get out of your head and own self-negative talks; the voices of those who have been influencing you.

So, when you create a goal for yourself, tell yourself and make sure that *"This is my goal, my own – not that of someone else*

— my own dream. I am not trying to live the dream of someone else. It is not one that is imposed onto me, not what my culture, my religion, my mentors, my superior tells me to achieve. I am not trying to live the life my father tried to have and that he missed, I am not forcing myself to do something that is not me. This is my goal, my own".

Inspired / insight / intuition

A lot of people set goals based on a thought process, of what is best (according to them) based on a somehow logical reasoning. Many call this "gut feeling" while it actually is only an "informed decision" built from their experience and buried in the back of their minds. Based on the past, it is therefore out of the present time and context.

The issue with this goal setting style is that the vision of the path to get there is already pre-defined and narrowed down to one or few potential directions. This limits the number of opportunities that one can create and prevents from seeing a bigger picture.

For instance, like I did want for a long time to be the CEO of a large company so that I could spread a coaching culture throughout the organization, imagine you have the goal of reaching a very high position in your organization, or another, from where you are. And imagine that you are already there, doing what you think you will be doing there and then. Imagine the people you will be working with, your superiors, you employees, the environment and atmosphere in which you will perform… what you see, what you hear, what you feel. How does it feel to you? Does it make you feel fulfilled, satisfied, complete, and whole? Do you feel that you are living your life and purpose?

If you cannot answer yes with certainty to all these questions, then this goal (or sub-goal) is probably not the right thing for you.

If you do answer with a resonating "YES!" to all these, then move on to the next point. If not, then you may want to go through the formulation of your goal again.

New

Differentiate, copy then tweak, make it yours. Even by the fact that you make it yours, that is, that you put your own spice and own twist into this goal, it becomes new.

Andy Warhol's paintings of *Marilyn Monroe* represent the essence of what *new* is. All the portraits can be said to be the same. However, they are not. The simple change in color makes them different from each other; each representing a new perspective of the same portrait, or person.

Some people will still argue this point, so I will ask the sceptics to imagine something totally new; an animal, a person, a landscape, an idea that has never been seen before. Now, if you break down this image, you will notice that it is made of pieces, however small, that already exist. But what makes it new is the combination in which you arranged the pieces together; in a unique and creative fashion.

The point here is that 2 objects, concepts, or ideas can appear to be the same, but the dissimilarity makes them different. Innovation does not have to be radical. A simple change of color, of tone, brings freshness to a product or idea. Hence the power of brainstorming. Ideas jotted down on a board, generating new ideas in a snowball effect, discussed and tweaked.

Napoleon Hill, in *Think and Grow Rich* talked about two forms of Imaginations:

<u>Synthetic Imagination</u>: a capacity to re-organize old concepts in a unique combination. The idea generation process of lateral thinking coined by Edward de Bono in *Lateral Thinking* and *Serious Creativity* is a tool that can assist in creating new, creative and innovative goals for oneself and one's team.

<u>Creative Imagination</u>: drawing from "hunches" and

"inspirations" received. This works automatically, provided that you let it happen. It does not require any efforts from your part. This relates directly to the previous points on MINE.

Excitement, Energized

The excitement that is felt when you are inspired is the self-measurement and indication that this goal or dream is actually in alignment with an experience that <u>must</u> be lived. Not as an obligation, but as a necessity for the world to bend and arrange itself... for you.

If it is the case, then this is very likely to be something that you need to do and go through, and that will make you become more successful. Not necessarily as a result, but in terms of learning and enrichment. This excitement does not guarantee the achieving of the goal, but it does guarantee the learning opportunities at your disposal for you to grab. Indeed, learning is an experience, not an achievement. And those around you who display the "been there done that" or "know-it-all" attitude are for sure those you will see in the same place few years from now.

Remember that this goal is yours, do not be bothered by what goes on around you. Give it your priority and full attention; this is what it takes, and do not wait on your colleagues for you to go for it. The whiners, the victims, the pessimistic and the like will only slow you down. They make you look back while running and make you lose your footing... and this may eventually make you trip.

Once you are energized, and excited about a goal, about an orientation, or even something good that is happening to you, do not slow down.

Once you look forward, it is then that you will see synchronistic events unfold before your eyes, and you will even be able to assist other colleagues or employees even more by demonstrating a life of strategic orientation and inspire them.

The book *Synchronicity: The Inner Path of Leadership* – J. Jaworsky & P. Senge relates the authors' path and career developments through a series of synchronistic events. These events and opportunities were there already before them regardless, but the authors could only see them for what they were because of their positive and opportunistic attitude and most of all thanks to the force of excitement that was driving them, to achieve their well-formed outcomes.

To recap, an effective goal needs to be so compelling that <u>it attracts you forward</u>, not push you from behind.

Fill the grid below in and see for yourself. Take any goal that you have set for yourself and feel the difference once you paint a picture that is clearer than the one you just "knew about". You will most likely feel energized, excited, even passionate about that goal and ready to go.

Criteria *Sample questions to answer*	**Description** of my goal by section
M – My goal *Whose goal is this? Who had the idea of achieving this goal?*	
I – Inspired /Insight/Intuition *I – Inspired, Insight, Intuition Did this goal come as a thought process or as an insight, an intuition? If it was a thought process, check it through your intuition. How*	

does it feel to imagine you already achieved it? *Do I feel inspired to reach this goal?*	
N – New *Is this a new goal, one that I have not heard about?* *How is it different from other goals?* *What makes this goal different and special?*	
E – Excitement /Energized *How do I feel about the prospect of achieving this goal?* *How excited am I about adventuring on the path to reaching this goal?*	

Conclusion

Goal setting is one those critical skills that makes the difference between an average manager and a great one. It is so important in fact, that I chose to put it as the first chapter of this book. As the old saying goes; You cannot manage what you cannot measure. I will add to that; You cannot reach your destination if you have no heading.

Giving a SMARTER and SMARTEST goal that is also MINE, to your team, to an individual or to yourself not only adds clarity to the direction one is to take, it also adds tremendous energy to the process. As you have very probably experienced by going through the exercise yourself, it gives such a laser sharp focus that it catapults the goal-goer straight to his/her success.

STRATEGIC FOOTSTEPS

Fortunately or unfortunately, we humans become more efficient when we have goals to reach. You are not left to wander around, but you have a direction you want to take. Have you ever tried to run with long stretches? You get tired very easily. If you, however, make smaller steps, then you can run very fast for a more extended period of time. Imagine now for a second if you had many little goals that have such clarity. You can have an abridged version of a goal that is SMARTER, SMARTEST and MINE for simple things. Say you want to have a report done. Are you usually procrastinating? Are you usually feeling uninspired? Are you more of an "ideator" and have difficulties executing? Are you a starter but have some difficulties to finish the task? So, imagine how formulating your mini-goals in such a manner will make you so much more effective, efficient and productive! Imagine completing anything you enterprise to do in a timely and effective manner. Imagine finishing whatever your superior asked of you in the most proficient way. Imagine helping your team members and subordinates complete their projects within the deadline you give them. How would that change your day, your week and your life?

Finally, I will leave you with this final thought for this part. Jim Rohn was sharing a discussion he was having with his mentor when he was 25 years old : "*[out of all the goals you set for yourself] Why don't you create a goal to become a Millionaire? Here is why; for what it will make of you to achieve it [...] The greatest value in life is not what you get, it is what you become*".

Technically, you could very well put the book down and be content with what you have learnt here and benefit tremendously from this first chapter alone. However, it is like the foundation of the building you want to build; it could be enough for you to live in the basement of your house, unless you want to build a skyscraper with many functional floors and rooms that will serve different purposes and that will give you much more space. This is only the first step of our journey to the top of the mountain, and like going on a trek, there is much more to cover and discover that will multiply the positive effects of this first step.

Andy Warhol's Marilyn Monroe's – 1962

CHAPTER 2.

WHERE AM I?

*HE WHO KNOWS OTHERS IS WISE. HE WHO
KNOWS HIMSELF IS ENLIGHTENED*
– LAO ZI

WHERE AM I?
UNDERSTAND THE CURRENT SITUATION FULLY

What is the use of a map if it is that of the wrong mountain? Imagine that, as you are at the bottom of the Annapurna Mountain, you have the map of Mount Everest. And what would be the use of having a map if you do not even know where you are located on that map, no reference point, no coordinates?

The past makes us who we are, right now, so it can be cherished, but it is not to be dragged because that will slow us down. You know, it's like you go on this trek in the mountain and you have to carry your super-large lenses camera to take all these nice pictures. If you are old enough you will remember having to carry also the extra film rolls. Don't carry so much luggage.

Where you come from, your culture, your education, your choices in life define you as you are now. Without the series of events and experiences that led us here, we would be completely different, as the Warhol's Marilyn's are. Had any one event been different, one decision, one deal, the entire situation, your job, your employees, your company would not be the same. If you take the time, even for one minute to reflect on this and the list of small yeses and nays that you have given in a day, and think on how the entire day would have been different had you said the opposite? And how this very moment, where you stand now as you read these words, would have been different – and probably would not even be reading this now, as I might not have had even written this book – only depends on this series of tiniest decisions and reactions you had throughout this period.

Take also your current job position; sure it is thanks to your competencies and experience, and knowledge... and how much does it rely also on the simple click of the "apply" button, the decision you made to Google for a job, the fact that you did pick up that phone, that you did set your alarm a bit earlier than usual, that you did take another route to the interview, the yes that someone down the line said to "you"?

This exercise might make you feel a bit dizzy or light-headed as you come to realize the immense impact of the smallest parts of your day or what otherwise appear to be insignificant events of little consequences. However, it is not for you to become fearful of your decisions and action, to be frozen and become inactive. Rather it is for you to realize that where you are, right now, in your career, in your position, the financial picture of your department, the state of mind of and level of motivation of your employees must be taken into consideration in the overall picture of *"where am I?"* map. *What brought you here will not get you there* – M. Goldsmith is another brilliant book that lays this out in much more details.

Be sensible to the external situations and influences that surround you, your department and your company. These are the factors that make the present precisely what it is. The politics that are more or less present in your company, the environment in which associates, bosses, peers and employees work in affect each and every one, directly or indirectly.

Einstein said *"You cannot solve a problem with the same mind that created it"*. This means that in order to be more effective in solving problems, you first need to change the way you look at things. "Take a step back" my father used to say, or like the Chinese proverb says: *"He who looks at a chess game plays better than the players themselves"*, and with a bird's eye view, you will change your perception of the situation. Only when you have a clear picture, map, of the current situation will you be able to design a clear road to reach where you want to go.

Johari window

Understanding how our communication and interactions with others I paramount to reaching our goals. For it is never a one man show.

The Johari window is a technique, a tool that is great to understand what is going on in your communication created by Joseph Luft (1916–2014) and Harrington Ingham (1916–1995) in 1955 . As a consequence it improves your level of communication, and reaction, it helps you lead and manage better, to perform better. This is about the perception people have about you as well as your own about yourself.

Quadrant 1 – The Open Self

There are things that you know about yourself, and that others know too about you; I am a man. I know that and people know that too.

Quadrant 2 – The Hidden Self
This is what you know about yourself, but others do not; *"You don't know everything about me, you know!"*

Quadrant 3 – The Unknown Self
This is where you have the things that people know about you but that you are unaware of. It could be some unconscious habits, things that you keep saying all the time, your body language, unless you start paying attention to yourself, raise your self-awareness, things that people notice about you that you do not.

Quadrant 4 – The Unknown Self
This is where the things people do not know about you, but you do not know either. It is outside everyone's awareness, or knowledge, even yours; I do not know about my future, and others do not either (apparently), I do not know about my medical condition because I do not go for check-ups, others do not either because they do not check me.

I would like to invite you to put bullet points, keywords in each quadrant that is respective to this area.

Which quadrant was the easier one to fill in?

Chances are it is either quadrant 1 or 2.

Proportionally, how many more have you written between Quadrant 1 and quadrant 2?

Now I have a question for you; do you remember a situation where you thought; *"If only he/she knew me better they would not say that, they would not judge me like that…"*? Well, what prevents you from sharing that information… and not be judged or not be told that?

Some say either that *"they did not ask for it"*… and they

still judge you, others say that they do not want to share that information.

So ask yourself; if you had given a little bit more information in that situation… what would have changed in the judgement? How would the entire situation – and the ripples of that situation – have changed? Maybe less harsh, maybe less judgmental, maybe less gossip about you. A gossip is some information that is not official. If it is official, then it is not a gossip anymore, it is a fact. So people start talking about something else… or someone else than you.

The question here is really: "*How much are you revealing about yourself to others?*" And you cannot complain about people judging, mis-understanding, mis-interpreting, gossiping about you if you do not share the information. Some whine about the fact that people talk about things they do not know about them… then tell them more! It is about what you <u>allow</u> them to know.

Moving the line between Quadrant 1 and 2 increases the amount of information that people know about you and reduce the amount they do not; it is about revealing yourself.

Moving the line between Quadrant 1 and 3 increases the information about yourself that you did not before knew; it is about improving your self-awareness. "Know thyself" was an inscription written at the over head of the entrance at the famous temple of Delphi in Greece. People were going to consult the oracle to know about what they should be doing in certain situation, about knowing their future… the answer was already there, right at the entrance of the temple: know yourself. This is all there is to do; just know yourself.

This tool is presented here only to bring to your attention that there are consequences of revealing… or not. There is no right or wrong; there are only consequences about what you are willing to reveal and to know about yourself. You have the choice, it is all in your hand.

Tony Robbins says that there are two pains: the pain of discipline and the pain of regret : *"If only I had done it"*. If you reveal information before anything happens… it might be tough, difficult or give a biting to your ego… because you do not want to. But you know that there are consequences for not sharing this information. And once it is done it is done, there is nothing you can do about it. The pain of regret, of the "what if" is the worst of the two pains.

It is up to you.

		I	
		Know	**Don't know**
The others	**Know**	*Quadrant 1* Known to me Known to others Open Self	*Quadrant 3* Unknown to me Known to others Blind self
	Don't know	*Quadrant 2* Known to me Unknown to others Hidden self	*Quadrant 4* Unknown to me Unknown to others Unknown Self

	I	
	Know	**Don't know**
Know (The others)	Quadrant 1 Improve Self-Awareness →	Quadrant 3
Don't know	Quadrant 2 (Reveal Yourself ↓)	Quadrant 4

VAK representation

It is commonly agreed that we have 5 senses; Hear, sight, smell taste and touch. NLP, Neuro-Linguistic Programing, a behavioral change and personal improvement technology with therapeutic effects was developed in the 70's by Richard Bandler and John Grinder . In order to simplify and categorize pattern recognition more easily, NLP grouped the 5 senses into 3, otherwise called VAK for short:
- Visual
- Auditory
- Kinesthetic

Kinesthetic comes from the Greek "Kine" and means motion. It relates to any physical movement but also to internal feelings as well. A person who is highly kinesthetic likes to touch objects but is also in-touch with his/her own body with a heightened awareness of it, the changes of temperature, their heart beats, how they breath, the different sensations that they feel in different parts of the body, like tingling in the feet,…

We use all these senses all the time, but we have the tendency to prefer using one over the others, primarily. It might be circumstantial, but there is one that comes in play more often or more easily. We use them all in a sequence. This goes so fast that we do not necessarily realize. For example, I see something that triggers a feeling reaction, which follows by hearing something. And this goes so fast that we do not necessarily consciously realize that process. And this can happen in any combination.

If I ask you what is the first thing you remember about you arriving at the very location you are now. Was it something you saw; people there or not, colors… was it something you heard or not, noise, people talking, silence… or something you felt; the temperature, the humidity, the wind on your skin…

As we said, it might be circumstantial, so I invite you to go through a series of questions so that you can identify what importance are each of the 3 senses Visual Auditory and Kinesthetic. In Appendix A, you will find a series of questions with each 3 possible answers.

Once completed, compute the number of answers you answered A, B and C so that you have 3 scores.

A is your score for Visual

B for Auditory

C for Kinesthetic

Your score does not mean anything. In the sense that there is nothing right and nothing wrong about it. As you see, you use all 3 senses. But there might be a sense that you prefer. There might also be a balance between 2 or even all 3 of them. This represents more flexibility for you.

For those with a higher score in Visual, you tend to remember things better visually, you tend to learn faster and better when you see the material. So when you would like to learn something new, I strongly encourage you to "look"; read about the topic, watch videos, DVDs, online, newsletter, watch people that you can model, mimic or copy. Emails are a great medium for people to communicate with you.

For those who are primary Auditory; stop emails! Stop right now. Go and talk to people. You will remember much better what the discussion was about you will retain information much better.

For those primarily Kinesthetic; you will remember better what you felt in the situation, how people made you feel, you will recall situations from the emotions attached to it.

As you have noticed in several of these questions; the language you preferred to use, words or expressions is directly linked to the sense you primarily use. This is because each of these 3 senses has its own dictionary... literally!

It is therefore highly important to understand which sense is your preferred one.

A person who is primarily visual uses visual words or expressions; talk about shades of light, the look, colors, *"It looks like"*, *"It is bright"*, *"It is clear"*, *"This person is colorful"*, *"Paint the picture"*, *"I see what you mean"*...my father, who is primarily visual, was asking for our attention while watching the news, by saying *"Watch what he says"* (*"Ecoute-voire"*) which technically does not mean anything. But this expression of his is brought about by the brain's preference to "see" the information while he was trying to convey that he consciously wants to hear what the person says.

A person who is primarily auditory uses words and expressions like: *"I hear what you say"*, *"Sounds good"*, *"Loud and clear"*, *"Let me hear you"*.

A person who is primarily kinesthetic uses words and expressions like: *"It's hot"*, *"I'm hot for it"*, *"How are you feeling today?"* *"Cool!"* By the way, "cool" is a temperature, related to kinesthetic... and I personally use it a lot.

So when you talk to someone and you pick up on the words that a person is using, one way of improving your communication is to use the same dictionary, even if it does not belong to the sense you primarily use. A trick to do this and build rapport very rapidly and effectively is simply to repeat the key words the other person uses. When Claudia (who is primarily visual) asks me how a dress <u>looks,</u> and I reply that she should <u>try it and feel</u> how it fits, there is miscommunication and obvious misunderstanding; we literally do not speak the same language. She feels misunderstood as she clearly does not see the behavior I should be demonstrating (all visual terms) and I feel she doesn't speak English. I let you imagine how this escalates!

When you conduct a meeting, a training or even a briefing where multiple people are present, you will no go around the room and ask each participant which sense they primarily use to ensure that everyone around the room understands and retains better the information you convey. You will not necessarily know who uses what. So use words from all 3 types of language. For instance, I use visuals, I move around the room, I use hand movements, I use my voice with different pitches, volume, tone, speeds, modulate the voice, and I also ask for interaction, I involve so that people remember better. In this manner, you ensure that each see, hear and feel the information that is communicated and that "talks" directly to them through the course of the interaction.

Reader or Listener?

Communication is the cornerstone to most relations and interactions. How many situations have you faced at work that originated with a miscommunication or a lack of clear or total communication? Unfortunately, we more than often fall victim of this shortfall... I rephrase: more than often we fail to establish a proper communication... which leads to unfortunate issues that could have been avoided otherwise.

In order to improve our communication, we have to identify what channel is the most effective to use.

We are either a reader or a listener.

Is it easier for you to read and retain information? Do you get easily distracted when the information is passed to you orally? Are you sometimes confused of what you think you remember hearing? You are most probably a reader. You might be an avid reader of books, articles, newspapers, magazines; this is the way you learn about your industry and market trends.

I am definitely a reader. I like to talk with my staff and colleagues, but when it is about receiving information or someone asking me to do something, it has to be done in writing. It happened very often that when my personal assistant was giving me a brief of my emails I got distracted by something I saw; a person passing by in front of my office, or even a fly. My brain switches off, it wanders around. My eyes shifted to the screen of my computer and my ears got shut. How many times did I have to ask her to repeat herself!

Therefore, if you are a reader like me, I would suggest you ask for the information in writing, if they want you to do something, ask for an email, ask for minutes of meetings and ask also for agendas of meetings in advance. This will help you prepare for the meeting rather than being put of guard with topics that you did not know would be addressed. Take notes. Once I explained this to my boss, after which, every time she was instructing me face to face to do something, she ensured that I was taking notes. If you are more predominantly a listener, then you remain more focused when the information is imparted to you verbally, you remember it more easily, and you will remember the words, the tone of voice also. When you receive materials in writing, you most probably switch off when there is too much to read, you may even not open the email at all. You might not be very kin on reading books, but you definitely enjoy talking with people.

In this case, I would suggest you schedule as many information meetings and briefings with your teams as possible. Also go and talk face to face with your boss or associates when following up on projects.

As usual, in communicating, and when talking about of communication style… it is about sharing your preferences with your colleagues. Let them know what works better for you. You see it is a partnership, but the responsibility is on you to tell others what you need so that the work relationship is more effective. Oh, and find out what works better for them too; communication is a door that swings both way!

Needs

Needs are what you perceive you must possess in order for you to feel happy, satisfied, for you to be performing at your best. In appendix B you will find a list of about 250 needs. Circle 10 of them that you believe are the most important to you. This might be the first time you do this exercise so I encourage you to be truthful to yourself, honest and open. You don't have to share this with anyone; this is for your own, personal growth. Once you have these 10 needs circled, rank them so that you keep only the top five most important needs for you. These five names belong to either one of the categories listed below. Identify which categories are the most important to you based on the top 5 needs that you have circled.

Now, the trick here is to realize that these needs might be slowing you down in your endeavor to reach your goals, your dreams. Ideally you would try to be need-less. In order to do so, it is very important for you to understand what it is that make you "need these needs".

Why do you have that need? I'm not asking "why" in the sense of whether they come from your family, or imposed upon by society, by your education, your environment, whether you've been forced to adopt them, etc. This would be highly important and interesting to learn from an information point of view and maybe would help you to realize how these needs emerged. However, the question here is *What is important for you about having that specific need?* The format of the questions is really important; *<u>What</u> is important for you <u>abou</u>t ...?* Otherwise, you run the risk of going into the origin of the need, as mentioned above, which does not serve the purpose of understanding how to be need-less. From there, drill down on that question several times by asking yourself the same question about the previous answer given. You will actually reach about a bigger and larger point of view of the importance you attach to that specific need.

For instance, if we take me as an example; I have a basic need of being praised. Let's imagine a conversation with myself:

Question: *What is it important for me about being praised?*
Answer: *It makes me feel that I am acknowledged.*

To be acknowledged is actually the category "Being praised" belongs to. Let's drill down further:

Question: *Why do I need to be acknowledged?* Wrong question, wrong format.

Answer: (Therefore the answer will not give you the information you need to move forward) *Well, I need to be acknowledged because throughout my education, my dad was not at home the entire week as he was spending his time traveling for work. My mother was taking care of us and I was not being acknowledged enough. I have this feeling that my sister was more taken care of and more given attention to than me... blah blah blah.*

But this is not the question you want to ask; the question should be formulated as mentioned before; *What is important for you about...?*:

Question: *What is important for me about being acknowledged?*
Answer: *It's important for me to be acknowledged because that gives me a sense of individuality.*
Question: *What is important for you about having that sense of individuality?*
Answer: *It is important for me because I want to be different.*

Now, you see the "need" becomes a "want" and that's what you want to achieve with this exercise. Going down deeper into the needs in order to realize what it is that you <u>want</u> will help you move from the position of a victim, with a need imposed upon you, to the position of power from which action can be taken in order to get what you want. So keep digging further:

Question: *What is important for you about being different?*
Answer: *Well it is important for me to be different because I don't want to be told what to do.*

In this example the "want" becomes a "don't want". Now, you will remember the "Wanter" and the "Avoider" orientations. The previous "want" (to be different) has now been turned into a negative "don't want" (to be told what to do) which puts me back again in the vulnerable victim position. Because I do not want it I would avoid doing certain things, situations, challenges, I would avoid making decisions and therefore I would avoid taking responsibilities also. So what you want to do at this point of time in the conversation, is to rephrase the negative "don't want" into an "I want" and reconstruct the same sentence into a positive form. So going back to my example:

Question: *What is important for you about being different?*
Answer: *I do not want to be told what to do...*
Question: *... Therefore what you <u>do want</u> is...?*
Answer: *I want to be free to do what I want to do, when I want to.*

And you can go on like this for a couple of other times asking again: *What is important for you about...?*

Now if we backtrack a little bit you see that my need of being praised is actually really about me wanting to make the choices I want, for what I want to do for myself. That puts me into such a position of power because now I know that if I want to achieve that I have to take specific actions and not be on the receiving end of the victim with "that's what I need and I can't do anything about it". This will take some time for you to go through this exercise for each of your needs, but I really encourage you to do it completely and thoroughly; it will change so much for you!

So to recap.
1. Identify a need.
2. Identify the category it belongs to.
3. Ask yourself: *What is important for you about having this need?*
4. Ask yourself that question for three or four times at each level.
5. When the "need" turns into a "want", remember to make sure that it is phrased in a positive form "I want" versus "I don't want".

Categories of Needs:
BE ACCEPTED
BE ACKNOWLEDGED
BE RIGHT
TO ACCOMPLISH
BE LOVED
BE CARED FOR
CERTAINTY
TO CONTROL
BE FREE
BE COMFORTABLE

BE NEEDED
HONESTY
TO COMMUNICATE
DUTY
ORDER
PEACE
RECOGNITION
WORK
POWER
SAFETY

Values

In a similar fashion as with the pyramid of Maslow, once you fulfill your needs then you can take care of the next level up, which are your values. Values are what you are attracted to. So first you need to attend to what you need before going into what you are attracted to. This organizes them in a hierarchical manner and promotes the natural prioritization to put "first things first".

Needs are in that sense what is called "hygiene factors". Hygiene factors are that which is very important to us but that we take for granted. They do not provide any additional benefits by having these factors, and all is good as long as we have them. However, we pay attention to them only when we do not have them anymore. This is the time when things go wrong.

Values are more like motivation factors. Values are your preferences, what attracts your activities, things, people's characters, characteristics and exercises. When these motivation factors are not there, nothing different happens. However, when they are present, they create additional motivation.

In appendix C you will find about 200 values. Circle the 10 that are most important to you. While going through this list you will see already what you're more attracted to, what you naturally gravitate around. Once you're done with these

10 values I would like you to rank them from the most important to least important. The most important would be the one that you are so attracted to that you want it right here, right now. And thus ranking the other 9 in proportionately reducing desire. Once you've done that, just retain the five top most important values of yours.

These define you and your behaviors.

Now let's take this a little further. If you sit back breathe and relax and think of a peak experience of your life, a moment where you felt so good, so excited, energized and invigorated, exhilarated. It may have been a fleeting moment or a long-lasting one. Think about it. *What was important about that experience for you? What value was honored during that experience?* Now, think of another time of your life when some event was so frustrating, annoying, angered you. *What put you in that state; what value was being neglected, or even violated?*

Find out for yourself if there is any relationship between these two examples, two peaks and valleys. *What is the common point between the value that is honored and that which is violated?* The value that is neglected is an even stronger one that you might have already selected as part of your top five list identified before, or maybe not. Check it out for yourself.

And now realize that whenever this value is not fulfilled is a critical moment for you. This is something that you cannot compromise on. If you do so you will feel very uneasy, you will feel not respected for who you are and you will feel ill.

This understanding and knowledge about your values and those that are most important to you is critical for you to start behaving differently. Do you usually <u>react</u> or do you <u>respond</u>? I want you to become responsible, response-able. And that comes with a deep understanding of who you are and where you are now.

Where is your center?

Stephen Covey wrote a very interesting book, one of many, called *Principle Centered Leadership*. In this great book Covey encourages you to identify your "center". What is important to you, what your constant focus, conscious or unconscious is on now. The types of centers that you might have could be your spouse, your family, money, work, possessions, pleasure, friends, enemy, your church or your religion, or you can even be self-centered. This concept actually complements what was discussed above about needs and values. Let's review them one by one and address the positive and negative sides of each:

Spouse-centered

If you are spouse-centered you are likely to put yourself at least second in your decision-making and your decisions criteria are primarily based on what your spouse says or asks you to do. You will see her direct or indirect influence in your work, your decisions at work, even your way of managing your teams. As we say: *Behind every great man there's a great woman.* The positive side of this is that you don't have to make all the decisions because they are somehow already made by your spouse! Directly or indirectly. The negative one is that your power is limited by the amount of power you give away to your spouse.

Family-centered

If you are family-centered your decisions are often based on family models or the traditions that you have received throughout your education. Your family does not have to be present for you to make the decision as they are already present enough in your mind consciously or unconsciously with what you have been dragging with you since your years of upbringing. You're leaving through your parents, through your caretaker, through the rules that they have imposed onto you. The good thing about this is that once again you don't have to make the decisions as we live through habits. Some people will say that they live by their own rules and this is fine, they have at least the guidelines and guidance often given or imposed onto them. The negative side of this is that it limits you in your own choices and decisions until you are aware of them and decide for yourself to keep them or shed them away.

Money-centered

If your center is about money you tend to look for profits in your decision making process. Profit can be monetary of course, but it can also be in terms of rewards. The positive side of this is that in the work environment, you might become a high-performing individual for your company. The negative side of this is that you might be restricted by looking primarily if not only at the financial aspect of the situations that you encounter, and limit your vision of yourself, your goals and direction.

Work-centered

If your center is about work, your decisions are very likely to be primarily based on your job, while putting aside other aspects of your life and environment; yourself, your mental and physical well-being, your family's and other relationships you may have, or not. The good thing is that you have potentially a fruitful and successful career because your focus is exactly there. The negative side of it is that your personal life is quite restricted to the demands, wants and requirements of your job. My dad used to say that *"Family is first, but work is more first"*. And by that he really meant that work was a tool that was a necessary evil, one that he enjoyed very much – and he was definitely a workaholic – but it was also a necessary tool for him to support his family. Although in his heart his family's well-being was primary, his actions were reflecting that work was the toll he thought was best to serve his goal. The point I am making here is that a center is really the one that is at the forefront of your actions. And it is very common for people to have their job as their primary center after only being a tool at first, which over time took over from the center that was the original focus of the person. Therefore it is important to realize that there is a difference between what your goal is and what you focus on.

Possessions-centered

If your center is around possessions you very often compare what you have with what others have or with what you do not have. It could be the job position that your former colleague or your former schoolmate have now with the job you currently have. And you are envious and jealous of them. And you wonder why they are in that position and why not you. You ask why they have the possessions that you do not have. The good thing about this center is that you can focus and find a way of motivating yourself in order to acquire more and find proactive approaches to achieve what you want. By comparing, the resilient who has grit will strive to get and do more in order to better his current situation. The negative side of this center is that you limit yourself to what you have not achieved and put aside the process of getting what you want. You waste time and energy in comparing and moaning about your condition rather than putting it to good use to excel and achieve your goals ahead.

Pleasure-centered

If you're pleasure oriented, your primary decision making process is around the positive things you get out of the options available to you. The good thing is that you are probably highly motivated in your endeavors because you know what you will gain out of them. The negative part of this is that you might not even have any or limited self-control. Indeed your decisions are primarily emotional, based on what your search for pleasure is directing you towards and you tend to lose your objectivity. Your focus is not on the long-term because you are be blinded by the short-term personal rewards. You are a victim and a pray to your own pleasures, somewhat like an addict.

Friend-centered

If you are friend centered you take into consideration primarily what people will think about your decision, about what you do and how you are perceived. The good thing is that you might end up being highly aware of what others think and adjust accordingly in order to win their hearts. You might have quite a high emotional intelligence. The negative thing is that you are likely limited to your social comfort zone and you restrict your options based on the opinions others might have on you. You are very likely to refrain from taking risks or being yourself for fear of judgement and alienation.

Enemy-centered

If you are enemy oriented you very often take into consideration what people might do to you, negativity speaking, and base your judgments and decisions on that. You will act according to what your enemies do. You will think about how you can protect yourself and your team, which is the positive side of it. The negative part of this center is that you end up with high limitations in your decision power because you take too much into consideration what can be done onto you rather than you achieving goals. You focus on the negative sides of the situations and might even tend to be paranoiac about what is going on to you, thinking that someone might be out to get you.

Religion-centered

If your center is around your church or your religion you are primarily guided by the belief in a higher power. You are very likely to look at the glass half full and surrender to the will of that higher power. The negative side of this is that you give up your power into an authority figure that is not you and therefore you might end up leaving things up to chance.

Self-centered

Finally, if you are self-centered you most probably self-referenced as mentioned earlier. You base your decisions on what you want, what you need and on what you feel is best for you. You are less dependent on other people's opinions and judgments and criticisms. The counter side of this is that you put complete trust in yourself by thinking you have the best ideas and best solutions. You do not take into consideration any other people's opinion, you might not work well in a team and you eventually alienate yourself.

Conclusion

Knowing where you currently stand is very important to understanding who you are now; how you function, what default modes your brain goes into in certain situations – especially during stressful ones – what your interests, your needs, your values and your points of focus are. These are the key criteria that define you as a person and that make you different from others.

At work, this knowledge of yourself will not only give you a huge competitive advantage over your counterparts and colleagues, but it will also improve your performance as an individual and as a team. Your colleagues, subordinates, superiors, teams and peers will also benefit from this as you will become more efficient, effective and even a source of knowledge and a resource to them.

Finally, by understanding yourself better, you will be

better equipped to understand others too, so that you as a manager or a leader will also be much more influential, powerful and respected.

In our trekking analogy, it is important to know what your strength, capabilities, your rhythm, if you can walk, run, jump, how often you need to take a breath... and if you go with other people in a group, you will be better off knowing what are the strength of each other. This is precisely what makes SWAT teams, SEAL teams and other Special Forces unit so strong; the fact that they are all different and complement each other in their sets of skills.

CHAPTER 3.

ROAD MAP

THE MAP IS NOT THE TERRITORY
– NLP PRESUPPOSITION

HAVE A ROAD MAP
PLAN AHEAD AND KNOW WHAT TO EXPECT

Now that we clearly know about the summit that we want to climb, that we have the correct map about the surrounding and that we know where we are on this mountain, now we need to figure out which direction to go. This is the time when you contemplate the different paths that you can take to reach the top. Ideally, you would have a guide. Even if I personally prefer to go on an adventure and trek in the mountain, I have been taught never to underestimate the mountain; the weather can change in a matter of minutes, the terrain can change with the temperature, something can fall from above, and a seemingly well-lodged rock can roll under your foot. So for our trip in the

Annapurna, Claudia and I had not only one, but two Sherpa (Sapta was an ex-colleague from work, and he brought along his brother). These guides knew the road beforehand, they had travelled it many time, and they knew the locals and the inn keepers too. Although I was disappointed about the only-2-hour-walk on the first day, I realized the next day that they clearly knew when it was best to travel and when it was best to rest. We can never say that someone knows the Mountain, but they knew the different ways to get "there".

People still confuse the two terms Mentor and Coach and use them interchangeably.

A Mentor is someone who is more experienced, generally more senior than the mentee and who guides by offering suggestions, based on his/her personal experience. A mentor can very well be a role model and will therefore be listened to more easily by the mentee.

A coach is someone who will only help those who want to be helped and those who believe that they can themselves take charge of the situation. He assists the coachee in finding his/her own answers through a series of appropriate questions that are relevant to the person, without imposing any of his view on the coachee, because the coach understands our differences and values our individuality, education, past, needs & wants.

All too often, people tend to impose on us their own views and "wisdom" acquired throughout the many years of their experience. How often have you seen or heard a person allegedly giving the advice to follow his footsteps because "I did it this way myself"? You might willingly follow someone who has achieved the kind of success you are pursuing for yourself, but to know fully well that your path might not exactly be the same – because that person is different, the circumstances were different, location & time, support or no support available at that time, the set of skills, knowledge and experience were different – is wise.

I have learnt so much that I feel the urge to share what I have retained. But when colleagues ask me what my biggest lessons were, I instantly reply: *"The biggest lessons I have learnt were not about what to do… they were about what not to do"*. I have very often put off projects until the last minute, not necessarily because I was procrastinating – though I have been guilty of that too – but because by discussing with people about their own experiences in similar projects, by learning from the hurdles they faced and the mistakes they made, I learn myself the shorter and more effective ways to complete mine. For instance, during my MBA, among the enormous amount of home projects we were generously given by our professors, one was about Excel, which, the professor warned us would take many, as in MANY, hours to complete over the following 3 weeks. The idea was to work on it and learn through trial and error new functions & tricks throughout the course of the following 20 days that would eventually help complete the project much easier. I was doing an apprenticeship at the time to finance my studies and I had literally half the time to do the same work that my classmates had. But I realized that those who had dived straight into the project the next day were discussing every day the struggles they were facing, and they were sharing their growing and increasing frustration for having to start all over again, several times. So over the course of the following weeks I had amassed such an amount of tricks, warnings and tips that I ended up completing the assignment in, literally, 10% of the time it took my classmates. To put in perspective, I had spent 8 hours in one go, while some of them averaged between 70-100 hours! This has taught me a lot about what to expect in the future and I still continue bypassing the quick-sands others got trapped into.

Although there is tremendous benefit in learning through your mistakes, and I still make a lot, there is so much that one can do alone… and there is so much more to learn from all the mistakes that each individual person around you makes.

Stephen Hawking titled one of his great books: *On the shoulder of giants*, adapted from Isaac Newton's *"If I have seen further, it is by standing on the shoulders of giants"*. To look ahead and to have a map of the road of the path that you want to walk is essential, and that can be given to you on a silver platter by mentors.

Mentors are an amazing source of knowledge and experience who can provide you with much guidance. The only thing to keep in mind is that their perception might be clouded by their own experience. Be aware of the beliefs they hold so that the same are not imposed upon you. For instance, I have heard many colleagues who were senior to me telling me that they had struggled for a number of years before reaching the position I wanted to get, and so I had to struggle too. The stories went that there are less than a few who had reached that position before a certain age, and so it is unlikely that I could do just that – especially since they themselves had not succeeded doing so.

Others were talking about a certain path you must (traditionally) go through in order to reach that position. Now, as soon as these people try to impose their own (negative) beliefs on me, I do not consider them as mentors, just as colleagues with a certain experience, and as a source of knowledge of what not to do. And believe me… I have learnt a lot!

Having mentors and finding mentors is a very important part of your path to success. These mentors can be found in your industry, in other fields also, they can be found in books. A mentor is a person who has already walked the way that you are embarked on. To follow these people will help you not reinvent the wheel, these people will help you see things in the way that you might not have seen before, they give you insights from their own experience, will tell you what works and what doesn't work, but remember this is for their specific point of view and personal situations. I found personally that books are an extremely important source of information: textbooks, business books, self-development books, ranging from articles business reviews case studies etc. Search for one, or two, or more mentors that can guide you. Each can have their specific skills set, experience, knowledge and wisdom. They may be living, or dead, or even fictitious characters. Some of my mentors are John Spence, Jerry & Marilou Seavey, Tony Robbins, Leonardo da Vinci, Derren Brown, Moriei Ueshiba (the founder of Aikido), even Master QuaiGon (from Star Wars)... to name a few.

Having a roadmap it is not necessarily about knowing what to expect but also to understand that what others have walked through is their own personal experience, the struggles they have faced are not necessarily the struggles you have to face; They may not have been ready for these struggles. Therefore, to understand their point of view will make you see these challenges in a different light.

The map is not the territory is another NLP presupposition that implies that each person's perception is at the base of the very reality they create for themselves. It is also obvious that our perception is different and from that stems that our reality also differs. This is a critical point to take into consideration for it realigns you with your personal life. You can live the life you want to live, not through the eyes of another, not the path that others have taken, but your very own. Your career, your shortfalls, the challenges you have faced as well as your successes have their own learning and wisdom to bring to you and to you alone.

Each fork is a choice that you can make for yourself. Your plan needs to be flexible enough so that you allow yourself to discover what is being offered to you as an experience. Take any city maps, or world maps, and you will see that even if there is only 1 road drawn, there are multiple options that are at your disposal to reach point A to point B. With that bird-eye-view, it is up to you to look deeply into that map and be aware that, to paraphrase the old saying: there are not only 1 road that leads to Rome.

Napoleon Hill talked about having a "Definite Major Purpose". Once you have defined what that is for you, that purpose that you strive to fulfil, you will be bound to look for options and solutions to go through, around, under, or above the challenges that arise as you walk on your path. Any challenges that you perceive to be can be seen from a different angle. The colleague who keeps being sarcastic with you in public, the boss that criticizes your every report, your subordinates that complain consistently about the work environment in the team that is under your supervision can all be seen as negative, as a challenge or as a feedback that you can overcome in order to continue on your way to success.

Claudia was suffering a lot in the last leg of our Annapurna trip. One of our Sherpa took on her backpack to relieve her from the pain that she had in the knees. She took the challenge to finish the trek. After our trip to Nepal, the pain continued for a long time and never seemed to go. Once examined, we discovered that she had Rheumatoid Arthritis, a generalized form of arthritis. The pain that she was having during the walk was real, tangible feedback that she was receiving from her body and that made us discover the condition that was still unnoticed at the time. This diagnosis was also a feedback from the body that pointed to yet another condition that had produced this arthritis in the first place. From then on, she knew what her options were to improve her condition.

Feedback is invaluable to one's development, don't wait for it. Ask for it.

CHAPTER 4.

TOOLS

GET YOUR TOOLS READY
KNOW YOUR STRENGTHS AND GET THE SKILLS YOU'LL NEED

"WHEN ALL YOU GOT IS A HAMMER, EVERYTHING WILL LOOK LIKE A NAIL TO YOU"
– POPULAR SAYING

Once you know where you are relative to your goal, where you are going and have the map of the path laid out in front of you, you could go and through yourself in. However, this is not effective planning, it's still not the most appropriate time to go yet. You now need to identify the tools that you will require in order to be ready for what lies ahead. Your plan needs also to be flexible, yourself need to be flexible. Like in Marital Arts, any part of the body, and by extension, anything around you can become a weapon (like in the Jackie Chan Kung-Fu movies). This means that any tool that you take with you can always be adjusted to your needs of the situation.

Not thinking about what tools you will need on your path to success and to achieving your goal is like taking your winter clothes to go on summer vacation at the seaside. So before we went off to Nepal for our trek in the Annapurna, we did a lot of research about the weather conditions, preparing our back packs carefully with the clothes that we would be needing, while paying very much attention to the weight (not for the plane, but because we had to carry them for the entire week). Do we need a tent, water metal bottles, cocking pots, cutlery, knife, torch? What about fire? Gas lighter, zippo, flint? Water proof poncho? What about water proof cover for the backpacks to keep the clothes dry? Does it ever rain in the Annapurna? Any medicine? How about altitude; how high are we going to climb? Do we need cloves maybe? Imagine for a minute that you do not have any of these items and that you do need them there. You would be attracting very unnecessary headaches for yourself. We say this is the 5 P's: Proper Planning Prevents Poor Performance.

There are different schools of thought regarding the effects of Strengths and Weaknesses on someone's performance. Some focus on the importance of understanding your weaknesses and working to improve them so that you become a "Jack of all trades". Others suggest focusing only on your strengths and disregard your weaknesses.

I prefer a more balanced approach that is even more effective: to understand your weaknesses so that you find ways to work around them, and that at the same time to grow yourself from the base of your strengths.

Coaching, and self-coaching, are very important techniques that help you identify the list of resources and tools that is best suited to your needs, preferences, abilities and personal outcome. *The book 28 laws of attraction* from Thomas J. Leonard is one of my top five self-development books. Leonard goes through a list of exercises of self-investigation to identify your own strengths. Understanding yourself is a key element to being strategic at work; knowing how you react in certain situations, knowing what makes you tick, understanding what processes your mind going through in certain situations while facing certain challenges is giving you a huge advantage that you can leverage in the workplace.

> In the famous Dao De Jing, Lao Zi said:
> *"He who understands others has wisdom*
> *He who understands oneself has clarity of mind"*

Understanding yourself is also a milestone in understanding others. You then can influence your environment and working conditions so that you can achieve what you want to achieve, reach your goals whether personal, for the team or for your company.

There are a number of sources of information that can help you grow your knowledge and put it in action. Knowledge is different than information. For me, knowledge is information that has been acquired and that is acted upon, whichever way to grow our skills. Skills are knowledge of "how-to", that you can bring anywhere with you, regardless of the position, that you can teach and transfer to others.

Many people I coach in the workplace are very attached to the outcome of reaching a certain position or level in the organization. However, when I investigate with them to understand what it is that they want to reach, specifically, what it is that is so important to them for reaching that position, and when I asked them what is it that they are going to be able to do once they are in that position or level, I and up with answers that have nothing to do with the position itself. People tell me that they will do this or that, that they will be able to do something else that they are not doing now. What they are really describing is a different behavior that the one they currently display, but that behavior is actually attached to a set of skills. I have been there too; for many years I was thinking only of becoming a General Manager in a hotel. Haven't you fallen in the same trap?

I ask them, and I ask you:
What if, by the time you reach that position, or right before you do, the company takes a turn and says that position does not longer exist? What are you going to do if you are so attached to the title of that position if you are only looking for a designation? And what will that position allow you to do that you cannot do now? What is that position going to bring you overnight, as a set of skills, that you cannot work on acquiring right now?

This is the moment when my clients realize that they can take action now, when they realize that it is not about the title and it is not about the position. Robin Sharma's book *The leader who had no title* refers exactly to that. The skills that you want to acquire do not have anything to do with the level in the organization that you are in or that you are going to reach.

Skills are merely tools, and your habits in using of them will define your behavior. We will go through the process that I used for myself; I made an inventory of all the skills that I already had, then I listed the skills that I wanted to acquire. Finally, I graded each one of them to the level that I perceived I was at in mastering them. This is a great way to give you a clear picture of the skills that you would like to develop further to achieve your goals, and those you would like to eventually master.

I invite you to do just that right now by making that

inventory of skills.
1. Just choose the skills that you are attracted to acquiring, whether it is for fun, or you have noticed that your performance would greatly improve had you had them.
2. Grade each of them from 1 to 10. 1 being I am a beginner, and 10 being I am a master at it.

You can refer to this list anytime and I invite you to do this regularly, at least once a month. By doing this frequently and regularly you will keep on recalling what your targets are and where you spend your time on to develop yourself. You will quickly see if your days are spent wisely, in alignment with the skills that your goal requires you achieve, or not. This will give you a tremendous focus on your personal development and by consequence will improve your work performance.

Some of these skills are:
- Social skills
- Communication skills
- Mathematical skills
- Facilitation skills
- Soft skills
- Hard skills
- ...

...and no matter what skills you are attracted to naturally will give you an edge in improving them.

You see, we learn naturally much better when we are curious and even better when we are interested (personal gain).

Once you know some key factors that are propitious to your growth, you will learn at an exponential pace:
- Know how you function
- Know how you learn
- Know how your brain functions

How do you learn?

We all learn differently. If we take the stance of constant learning, you should find out which way is the most effective for you; by watching, by hearing, by reading, by doing or with a mix of them. This will help you to learn faster and to better retain the information. By acting on the knowledge acquired, it will transform itself into a skill that you physically acquire and understand. It migrates from an intellectual knowledge to a physical, almost visceral, understanding.

For instance, when I decide to focus on a particular skill, I find all the material that I can and that is appropriate for me (written) and I learn as much as I can. For at least a week I read everything I can; articles, books, newsletters, I watch videos on YouTube, on Twitter & LinkedIn posts, I attend seminars, online webinars and saturate myself with information so that it syncs inside both my brain and body. In karate you practiced the same move over and over and over again 100's and 1000's of times until it becomes part of what you do. It becomes instinctive and it builds up into what is called muscle memory.

Your brain is also working in the same fashion; like a muscle, it retains with practice. It manages to repeat the information and transform it into knowledge and even applies it in different contexts, which increases the flexibility of usage of that skill. The brain is flexible, malleable… and it is all "a brain thing".

What competitive advantage you will get over your colleagues and peers, what will make you stand out of the crowd of your colleagues and team, what will make you shine in front of your boss are mostly the skills that you have acquired and use, and the personal development that you have gone through. Whatever you have applied to help yourself, your boss, your colleagues, your team and your company will be what is remembered of your impact and positive influence on others.

To be strategic about yourself is also about being strategic for your environment and your surroundings; the environment mentioned in previous chapters. By you developing your skills and filing your toolbox will definitely make anyone else look less successful, shine less, be less noticed or attractive, and you will probably become a threat to your peers and even to your superior. So you have somehow to become like a mushroom that grows in the moist and in the dark, in the shadow and under the protection of the oak trees, patiently but surely becoming a truffle, a precious culinary gem, that wherever it is used will enhance the dishes and bring them to a whole other level.

So my point here is for you to achieve the goals that you set for yourself; focus on your strengths so that you can grow, leverage them and differentiate in order to build your competitive advantage. Do not discard your weaknesses, understand them, work on them, but only so much that you are able to face the challenges that you might encounter with these weaknesses. However, your time should be well spent on growing yourself from the strong foundations of the skills, knowledge and strengths that you already process. It is somehow like becoming a specialist.

Reflect upon your own industry, company, and department. There are specialists, and they are there for reason; they all have their purpose and role to play. The skill of bringing people together and leveraging the strengths and specialties of each individual in your team and of those around you is therefore of paramount importance. Of course the cynical who only look at the negative will see this as using the strength of their colleagues to do what they cannot do and envy them. In any discipline, any team player, any martial artist and any army commando will tell you the same thing: they harness the opportunity that presents itself to them at any given time. They are actually looking for opportunities. And whatever challenges they face they know that a solution is around. The solution might not be within themselves but it is around them in disguise in the shape of a colleague or skill that they can acquire or a book or any other material for that matter. Any martial artist reaching the level of mastery in any discipline although as the front one another will tell you that it is not about the move anymore it is about adopting that move to the Sikkim stances. Flexibility of the brain is inherent to the organ why not be flexible as a behavior and adopt tweak those skills to use them in different situation and circumstances. Why do we have so many different points of view about the same situation? It is because of the interpretation. Remember the map is not the territory. Your reality is only yours to have and is only your perception of the second stances around. Your superior appearing to be bossy is only your perception. How come your colleague is not perceiving the same thing? It is only a point of view. The ability to change your point of view to put yourself in the shoes of another also called empathy of looking from different perspectives is also a skill that is vastly important and far-reaching when used properly. It will give you a different perspective of things a different understanding and you will stop seeing solutions appearing by miracle. The good thing about skills is that it is never too late to learn and by bringing focus to those skills you want to acquire those you are attracted to curious about will help you in your carrier.

See the Appendix for a self-assessment of skills

Strengths & Weaknesses

This is a basic question that recruiters ask very often. Can you list your top 10 strengths and 10 of your weaknesses? Making an inventory of our capacities and challenges is part of knowing where we are.

MY STRENGTHS	MY WEAKNESSES

Some of your findings might be surprising to you… or not, but having this knowledge in the back of your head and being consciously aware of this will be quite different to you now.

Now, it might sound quite crazy, but I suggest to focus only on your strengths. You might see this as being counter-intuitive, at least from the point of view of what you have been told for years.

But, bear with me and hear me out.

Consider these strengths and weaknesses on a scale of 1 to 10, 1 being the most disastrous level of efficiency of the weakness and 10 whereby you are what you would consider an expert. If you were to put them all on the same scale, as the below example shows, it would look something like this (Each letter would represent a strength of weakness):

A	10	STRENGTH
B	9	STRENGTH
C, D, E	8	STRENGTH
F, G, H, I	7	STRENGTH
J	6	
	5	
	4	
Q, R, S,	3	WEAKNESS
T, U, V, W	2	WEAKNESS
X, Y, Z	1	WEAKNESS

In this example, you would have 2 different clusters of points that are strengths (top scores) and bottom ones (lowest scores). There might be one that is actually lower than the others (J) and there you might not see it any longer as a Strength.

Anything in between these 2 clusters are neither strengths nor weaknesses. They are there, you possess them, they are not really an asset of yours, but they do not bother you either.

When people talk about working on your weaknesses, the result is not to transform a handicap into a strength, it is merely to move it to a non-bothering inconvenience (between weakness and strength).

If you were to consider how much better you would be at your work if you were to grow one of your weaknesses by 1 level. How would that impact your productivity? And how much effort would that take from you to lift that up by 1 level?

Now, if you were to consider how much your productivity would improve if you were to work on one of your strengths so that it improves by only 1 level; what difference would that make for you? For your boss? For your colleagues? For your team? For your company? And how much effort would that take from you to lift that up by

1 level?

Finally, if you were to compare the ratio effort/impact of growing a weakness by 1 level with the same ratio of working on a strength, what would you prefer to work on?

In conclusion, once you know your weaknesses, just plan your work around them, avoid them. Focus on your strengths, they will grow very rapidly because they are already there. They only need a bit of tweaking to create a result that is compounded.

Habits

As the saying goes; We are creatures of habits. The great book *The power of habits* – Charles Duhigg will change your views on what a habit can do for you, and you will no longer look at them as being negative only.

Tony Robbins talked in one of his videos of a very simple and highly potent way of changing your habits (he calls them "rituals") with only 4 questions:

What do you want to improve? How is it like currently? – Be specific

What are the rituals (habits) that brought you here?
What do you want? – Your vision – Be specific
What are the rituals (habits) that will bring you there?

Motivation

Self-referenced or Externally-referenced?

It is important to understand what motivates you. In this section, I am not talking about what interests you, I'm talking about whether you are self-referenced or externally-referenced. A person who is externally-referenced is somebody who is motivated by reward, praise, a pat on the back, a compensation etc. Unlike what we think, it is not necessarily bad to be externally-referenced, it can be used to your advantage, because when you know what motivates you then you know what to look for to be motivated.

A person who is self-referenced is somebody who is

primarily motivated by his or her own success that he or she will be the sole judge of. This person might be perceived as being very independent, very forceful, strong, and stubborn and all the rest of it. But it can also be highly important to be self-referenced in some cases for you will not take criticism too personally.

Ask yourself: "*How do I know that I am successful in what I endeavor? How do I know that I am performing well? How do I know that I did my job and I did it well?*"

A person who is externally-referenced will say something like: "*Well, I see the numbers, I see the results, I see that we are above budget, I hear my boss tell me that I did a good job, I receive congratulations, I see my teammates happy, I see positive guest comments, or I do not hear any complaints.*"

A person who is internally-referenced will not be thinking too much. The reply will come out very promptly: "*I just know*".

Once you know what your reference point is (or what your colleagues' points of views are) just by asking yourself these simple questions, then you will be able to ask and demand what it is that motivates you, so that you can be even more motivated than you are currently.

Tools are not necessarily yours to have; you may look for people who have the tools that you need. Colleagues, peers, mentors are also resources that you have at your disposal. However, it is up to you to collect these resources and utilize these to your advantage.

For projects, you may want to build the team of people who have the inventory of tools you require in order to hit the mark. It works in the same principles as DeBono's *Six Thinking Hats* that represent six different points of views of the same topic, 6 different thinking processes, namely;

- White hat for Facts,
- Yellow hat for Positivity, Value and Benefits,

- Black hat for Judgement, the Devil's advocate
- Red hat for Feelings, Hunches and Intuition
- Green hat for Creativity, Possibilities, Alternatives
- Blue hat for the Thinking Process, ensure the guidelines are observed.

For your personal growth, development, for your path towards achieving your goals, the resources that are available to you will serve you in many ways: to use temporarily, to learn from, to acquire permanently… and use them in all the combinations possible.

In summary, whether you consider resources, tools, or people, putting them together, the overall is more than the sum of its parts. This is also the meaning of the abbreviation of TEAM: Together, Everyone Achieve More. When on the mountain, this is the main reason for guides to beg people to go in groups. First; each can help another in emergency situations, and also for moral support; When you are alone, your mind can turn out to be your worst enemy. Second, each person will bring different skills or ways of thinking that can get the entire group out of very dangerous situations.

Now that we finally have our goal set, the right map, the tools & the resources, now that we know where we are and where we are going, we are ready to go.

Let's move.

CHAPTER 5.

FIRST STEP

*A JOURNEY OF A THOUSAND MILES BEGINS
WITH A SINGLE STEP*
– CHINESE PROVERB

MAKE THE FIRST STEP
GET GOING

A national survey was completed with 4,000 senior US executives to answer a major question that impacts all businesses: what inhibits execution? Here are the 4 reasons given, with their respective percentages of respondents:

1 – Holding onto the past/unwillingness to change (35%)
2 – Economic climate (29%)
3 – Company culture (23%)
4 – Inability to work together (21%)

It is essential to act on our goals; all the planning, the

wishes, the hopes, the help & push can be present, and yet, nothing gets concrete because you do not DO anything about it. How many people do you know who want to achieve things but do not take any actions about it? There are just at the foot of the mountain, they know what they want, they know where they are, they know what they "have to do", they are full of "I know I should… but" … but they do not act on it.

In the beautiful book *Execution* – L. Bossidy & R. Charan argue that execution is the number one thing Leaders commonly lack. *"Do the thing and you shall have power"*, said Ralph Waldo Emerson.

The only difference between a dreamer and an achiever is Action. You can dream as much as you want, you can plan as much as you want, you can fantasize as much as you want, you can talk as much as you want about what you desire, but unless you act, nothing will happen. And it is about <u>you</u> doing it.

Shantideva a mystical teacher of Ancient Tibet said *"Why worry if it can be remedied? And why worry if it cannot be remedied?"* This is really about what you do about the challenges you are facing. The people I coach often have issues with others. Some would like others to behave differently, some would like to have them stop behaving in certain ways, and some would simply like for things to be different. And my only reply to them is equally simple: *"What do you do about it?"*

The number one thing that most leaders lack is execution. The great book *Execution* deals exactly about this key differentiating skill that make the difference between the top leaders and CEOs of the world, the achievers, and the rest of the crowd who keep on complaining. Procrastinators in the workplace – although they might have deeper negative believe systems or personal issues that prevent them from taking action – face exactly this challenge: they do not start. You might have heard the common idiom that says that: *"When you feel sad, start working"*. And there is some wisdom in it. Another one says *"Appetite comes while eating"*. Interestingly enough from a psychological perspective, depression is also treated through action.

In my experience in all the departments that I have been working in, I have conducted countless brainstorming sessions that were aiming at identifying growth opportunities for the companies I was in. the results showed exactly the same trend, the same shortfalls.

Out of 100 ideas that were formulated through brainstorming, I would say that roughly only 10% of them were acted upon. And I do enjoy this creative process because our brain works so much faster than our body. It hones the power of working as a team, of compounding ideas on each other's. Everyone has great ideas even the janitor working in the basement of your building has ideas on how things could be dealt differently. But how many of them are implemented? How many people do you hear complain or report incidents without coming up with solutions? Only those who succeed did take action.

A story says that when Napoleon Bonaparte reached heaven he asked God who was the greatest leader in history. God replied: *"Your gardener"*. *"How my gardener was the greatest leader in the world?"* Replied Bonaparte, furiously. *"Well"* said God, *"Had he gone into the army he would have been the greatest leader in history"*.

In order for you to start taking action more often on the ideas that you generate, you have to understand yourself better. You can also learn from others; look at your colleagues, look at those who have ideas and who talk a lot with *"If I was... I would"*. Investigate, get curious, and ask them why they do not. You will learn a lot about procrastination… and how creative people can be at making excuses. If you are lucky, they will tell you what really holds them back. Is it certain beliefs, cultural barriers, self-negative talk, habits or education, fear? And ask yourself if you not taking action more often stems out of similar reasons. Beware if you want to be strategic and make a difference or to differentiate yourself in the workplace, you will have to be honest with yourself. And as Yogi Berra said *"If you don't know where you're going you'll end up somewhere else"*.

Understanding how you make decisions, how you choose to go for it or not, will make a tremendous impact on your own performance and on that of your team. That will make you differentiate yourself from the group of dreamers as you become an achiever. Understanding if you are more of an "Avoider", which stands that you are looking more at the potential challenges avoiding issues, troubles, pitfalls, difficulties etc. or a "Wanter", meaning that you are looking forward to achieving & reaching goals, will make you understand better your own behavior and that of your colleagues around you.

There is no "better" characteristic between "Avoider" and "Wanter", there is only the understanding that allows you to optimize your decision-making process. Remember that it is about understanding yourself, knowing your strengths so that you can leverage them.

In combination to this approach to situations of "Avoider" and "Wanter" is another dimension that is critical to action-oriented people and that makes the difference between a "Thinker" and a "Doer". Again here, there is no better one than the other; there is only the understanding of how our brains work and how different we are.

A thinker is somebody who needs to think a lot, to reflect on the pros and cons. A doer is somebody who is more likely to get his head down and start running. They might even do the acting before thinking. There is no right or wrong, there are only consequences. A thinker will take more time before acting, but thinking does not imply that the person is going to act or not. However, he is more likely to be a procrastinator.

A doer is more likely not to think too much of what lies ahead and therefore might not be as strategic as a thinker. In the 90's we were talking a lot about B action movie heroes who were hitting the bad guys and then reflecting upon their past actions. This is very often a common trait of doers… at the extreme.

Now that you're reading this book about strategy and how to apply a strategic approach for yourself in your work environment, you might be a doer because you took it upon yourself to act on what you wanted to achieve by reading on this topic. You might also be a hard-core doers, although very aware of your "condition" ☺ but who would like to be a lot more strategic and add weight to your thinking before acting so that by applying these techniques you will take action in an even more efficient way. However, if you are very much interested in theories, in concepts and not necessarily concerned about applying them, just to add to your library of ideas, then you certainly are a thinker.

It becomes very interesting when you put these two dimensions into a matrix. Combining the "Avoider" and the "Wanter" with "Thinker" and "Doer".

In the grid below these two sets of aspects are combined:

	Avoider	Wanter
Thinker	1 Procrastinator	2 Yes but
Doer	3 Start-Stop	4 Go for it

In quadrant one a person who is primarily "Avoider", avoiding challenges and also a "Thinker" will very

probably be a procrastinator. In the opposite quadrant, number 4, a person who is a "Doer" & "Wanter" has goals will act immediately without pondering on future challenges or issues and will just go for it.

Where it becomes a lot more ambiguous is when in quadrant number 2, somebody has goals and he is "Wanter" but is also a "Thinker". This is somebody who is a lot more strategic about the goals that he wants to achieve and will therefore take the time to evaluate, hopefully not for too long, before taking action because he knows that he has a goal to achieve; he has a target.

In quadrant number 3 you will find somebody who is a doer, but who is also avoiding. He tries to avoid issues, which counteract his actions. It is liken to somebody walking backwards towards his goal, or somebody always driving on first gear, alternating between the gas and brakes pedals.

When you manage a team or when you do teamwork, I strongly suggest and recommend that you do such an inventory of each of your colleagues so that you know better what type of characters you have around. Now, you don't necessarily have to go and ask them questions one by one. Although you could. You can also identify their location in this matrix only by reflecting on and analyzing their behaviors. The language they use also strongly reflect the quadrant in which people are in that matrix.

When a new team member joins your organization or when you yourself join for the first time, an honest discussion with your future teammates to identify who is where in this matrix would bring you a tremendous advantage in your future relation with your colleagues. By doing this myself with my new joiners, in five minutes

I could identify what works better for that person so that I could delegate the exact tasks to that individual so that the process would be a lot more fluid, speedy and effective. This had a direct impact on the performances of several of our teams and departments as a whole. These five minutes of my time made the person in front of me feel understood and valued for. With few simple questions to identify these orientations, we connect together like no other manager achieved after months of arguing and frustration for not getting what he expected from his team members before me. This is but one tool that I'm giving you here in order for you to maybe feel more confident in making the first step with your colleagues. And that might be the most important one of all.

While putting a team together for a project or in a more permanent situation, a very strategic way of taking the first step is to gather a mix of all characters tapping into all quadrant. This will give you a wide range of perspectives that will make your project more effectively ran to completion. Imagine for a second that you knew exactly where your colleagues were in this grid. You would be able to attribute and delegate the appropriate portions of the project to the person who has the mindset that serves that specific part better. In a design thinking approach you would ask a person who is in the quadrant one to do the brainstorming. In the last step of design thinking called prototyping you would assign somebody who is in the quadrant number four. You now have a person who thinks about all the issues that can occur and that need to be avoided (quadrant 1) a person who has the buy-in to achieve the common goal but needs to think first (quadrant 2) a person who will play the role of a motivator and kick-start things (quadrant 3) the person who will execute and make sure the goal is reached (quadrant 4)... project completed.

CHAPTER 6.

FORGET

IN THE LAND OF THE BLIND, THE ONE-EYED MAN IS KING
– DESIDERIUS ERASMUS

FORGET THE GOAL
FOCUS ON WHAT'S IN FRONT OF YOU

Having a goal, a target, a mission statement, and reviewing it, reminding yourself of them is something, but keeping that goal in mind all the time can take the place of blinders. If the goal has really been defined to be SMARTER, SMARTEST and MINE, then the goal is already there in your mind, in your heart, deep down, you are the goal, like breathing; you do not need to think about it.

Now, I will suggest something that you will first think of being counter-intuitive: forget about your goal.

By forgetting about your goal, your mind can be put to other uses.

Some colleagues I have worked with used to learn so many numbers by heart that it became impressive to most. But their mind was so busy remembering these that they could not recall other events or conversations that occurred and that happened to be even more important. I have learnt that at work, I need not recall everything, as long as I know where to find the information. I have also grown a belief that whatever it is that I need to know at any given time, I will remember it. By teaching this to my teams, I have shown them that they can free their minds and use it to much greater extent and apply it to many more areas, so that they became more creative, more insightful and more innovative in finding business solutions.

Once upon a time in ancient Japan, ladies used to wear very delicate long dresses made of the finest silk called Kimono. There was a time when 2 monks, the master and his apprentice were walking through a forest, practicing mindfulness and silent walk as part of their daily rituals. Once approaching a muddy river, they encountered a lady standing by the bank puzzled on how to cross it for the bridge was broken. When asking the monks if they could help her cross, the master did not consider for a second his vows of chastity, which include touching any females and he did not hesitate to take her in his arms so that she would not soil her beautiful kimono. After crossing over the muddy river, the lady was very grateful to him. And after a couple of hours of meditative walk, the apprentice finally broke the silence;
- *Master, how could you take that lady in your arms, this is outrageous, this is against our vows, this is against the tradition of our school, and against our rules, how could you?*
- *Well, my young apprentice, I have left that lady at the river a while ago, but it appears that you are still carrying her.*

All this time, the apprentice had been keeping in mind

what his master had done hours before. Can you imagine what that poor apprentice must have gone through in his head, all this time? And can you imagine what he had been seeing on his path while walking? Only the master carrying the lady... nothing else. He might have not seen anything of the beautiful scenery that they were walking through, he might not have smelt any of the sumptuous scents that come to him, not noticed any of the charming sounds of the birds chirping about, not have felt anything of the breeze that was cooling his sweat. And this was his making of his own torment and demise.

How many times have you driven and arrived at your destination (hopefully with no incidents) but you did not remember at all how you did? How scary is it to realize that you have not been conscious of anything happening around you, cars, trucks, motorcycles and all, for such a long time? Especially when you know that an accident can happen in the blink of an eye. You were too preoccupied by what you had to do, by what had happened before you left. And you missed the world that was around you. Christopher Reeve (Superman, the old one) who became quadriplegic after an accident while horse-back ridding said to Larry King about the event: "(horseback riding) *is a partnership. And the lack of communication -- one of us got out of sync* [...]".

Not being present when you do something can do that to you. Well this is a bit of an extreme case, but you get the gist; keeping and holding something in your mind too tight takes away your awareness of the opportunities that are around you. I recall having meeting with colleagues from different properties, and some of them were so focused on doing better than the competitors that hours were spent on reading their own results, and how they positioned compared to their competition, and compared to the sister properties, and how they are compared to last year,... and on, and on, and on. And so they were satisfied with a marginal growth, or a softer drop than what those around were suffering from. Until the competition beat them to it. And they started losing share at a much faster pace than the market. Sure there was arrogance in the success, and there was patting on each-others' shoulder but when I quoted Waren Buffett "You need to be cautious when others are greedy, and be greedy when others are cautious" the only comments were about how the market was falling (2015). So there was satisfaction and comfort in the fact that we were not the only ones suffering. It seems harmless to compare yourself with others, but once this attitude becomes dominant, that this attention to others becomes the predominant one in your business, it pervades the team's focus and eventually kills the company from within. Dictums remind us all the time *"Always be on your toes"*, *"Always have the eye on the ball"*, *"Run your own race"*, *"Always prepared"* (the Boy-scouts' motto), *"Be mindful"*, *"Be ready"* & *"Mind the gap"*…

Having the goal always in mind has the exact same effect. You walk with your head high, looking up at what you want and you do not pay attention to were your feet go. Remember missing a step down, thinking that the floor was flat? Back on the mountain side this is a very dangerous way to walk on the terrain; any slight change in the ground condition, slope, a hole, a shaking ground, a lose rock, any step can well be your last.

STRATEGIC FOOTSTEPS

CHAPTER 7.

ENJOYMENT

ENJOY THE RIDE
HAVE FUN!

Has it ever happened to you to be in such a passionate discussion that you forget all that is around you, the original purpose of the conversation or even the agenda? That is the time when you are the most prone to follow your intuition, to go with the flow, to be in "the zone". And that is the time when you enjoy the conversation so much that the level of attention goes beyond the mind and reaches the heart. This is the time that your learning reaches a deeper level that imprints in our entire body and can be recalled any time. This is when you have fun.

Although this will not do justice to the entire book, I will summarize what Mihaily Csikszentmihalyi, the renowned psychologist who studied creativity, happiness and the state of *flow* wrote in a book under the same name . This will give you the gist of his message. "Flow" is a state of mind in which we are all at some point of time, when we perform a task with such ease, grace, harmony that we completely forget everything else. Athletes call it "to be in the zone". This state is accessible when there is a balanced, proportionate amount of challenge for the amount of corresponding skills at our disposal.

The below graph illustrates it.

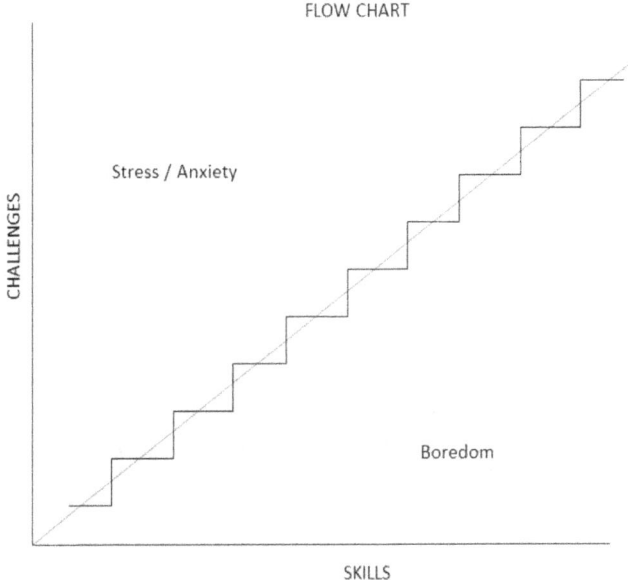

Inspired by Mihaily Csikszentmihalyi's *Flow*

When you face too many challenges – for a particular task – there is stress and anxiety. This happens mainly because you do not have the amount of skills to balance the amount of challenges. Conversely, when you have too many skills, when you are "overqualified", you are getting bored. In either state, this generates underperformance. The goal is to increase ones skills or acquire new ones that are appropriate for the task at hand when there is too much challenge, and to look for more challenge when one has too many skills. First, by doing so, an employee would display a very positive attitude with a willingness to learn new things/skills, rather than giving up. Second, that employee would display a proactive approach to his superiors by taking on additional responsibilities. Either way, the employee will be seen as being a lot more of an asset than the one who remains idle because of too much challenge and stress or over-skilled. Once the balance is achieved between skill and challenge, there is pure enjoyment happening, creativity, and fun.

Unfortunately, there are many people who are so serious about what happens to them that they become dragged and caught up in the events of their lives that they do not see the end of it and end up being cynical. Which do you prefer to be? The choice is yours.

You will find a lot of useful insights when reading *Don't sweat the small stuff*.

One of the questions that I took from the book and that I ask myself very often is: "*Will this still matter in one year from now?*" This question has help me get so much perspective on things and events, that I enjoy them a lot more. Just try it for yourself, and have a look at the other suggestions, one will for sure resonate with you and help you see things in a different light.

Children are beautiful because they are true to themselves. They are so congruent because they do not try to pretend to be someone they are not, they have not suffered the pressure and oppression to be someone else, they are just who they are. Why are they so beautiful, even when they are angry? Because they are Anger itself. They are Joy, they are Sadness, they are Anger, and fully embody the emotion that they feel at the time. Adults become ugly because they try to fit in, they try to hold themselves back.

STRATEGIC FOOTSTEPS

I still remember a time in the Parisian metro, coming back from work. I was reading something that made me laugh out-loud, and when I lifted my head, I saw the scornful looks all around, almost saying "*What is wrong with you?*". It is now even taboo to laugh in public... how low have we fallen?

Something that might surprise you is that opposite emotions are equally strong. Like a pendulum, they will swing to one side as high or low as they will swing to the other side. Bashar (Darryl Anka) says that Emotions are E-motions, really they are "Energy in Motion". Consider this; how much anger have you been repressing inside, and for how long? On the count that it is not appropriate to show emotions – especially not the negative ones – at work, in public? And how often to you let some steam out? How burning and powerful are these geysers of anger? Are they not hurting your colleagues? You?

For the longest time I used to deeply bury my frustrations and anger. I was so good at it that I even believed that I did not feel anything bad. Until it came a point that I could not hold it back anymore and anger started to come out. Like a cooker-pressure it had to get out. In small but highly intense bursts I would blow out on people in disproportionate manners. I literally became a danger to others and to myself. Until enough was enough, it all came out, like the top of a volcano exploded sending rocks and fumes a thought feet in the air. The energy was so strong that I furiously went shadow boxing for about 1 hour nonstop, then still filled with anger wanting to come out, I left for a 2 hour run, climbing the hills of the vineyards outside the house. I am not sure you see what they look like, but we are talking of an elevation of 50 meters per 10 meters horizontally, that is a 500% inclination, almost 80 degree angle! This is the power of emotions. Now you can use these emotions negatively or positively. Imagine what you can achieve with such a rush of energy that last for such a long time.

Now, even if our mountain is Mount Everest, what is the point, really, of taking on the challenge to reach the summit if we do not go with the intention to enjoy the trip?

This section is proportionately short because it can be summarized by these beautiful words that have been used, re-used, adapted and paraphrased so much so that we do not know the exact origins precisely; *"Life is not measured by the number of breaths we take but by the number of moments that take our breath away"*.

PART II

ESSENTIAL KEY NOTES

THE DEVIL IS IN THE DETAILS
– POPULAR SAYING

CHAPTER 8.

WANDER

[...] SHE RAN ACROSS THE FIELD AFTER IT, AND FORTUNATELY WAS JUST IN TIME TO SEE IT POP DOWN A LARGE RABBIT-HOLE UNDER THE HEDGE. IN ANOTHER MOMENT DOWN WENT ALICE AFTER IT, NEVER ONCE CONSIDERING HOW IN THE WORLD SHE WAS TO GET OUT AGAIN.
– LEWIS CAROLL, ALICE IN WONDERLAND

IT'S OK TO GO ASTRAY… OPPORTUNITIES COME

When I was travel alone in other countries, I used to have a plan of all the places that I wanted to see, then run through the places. Of course my schedule was so full that I hardly so anything in each place, they were just stops. Over the years, I realized what I was missing; the opportunities to discover the life the locals were leaving. That meant that I would go to some places that most tourists never see. I would just walk the streets and wander around. I have discovered the most amazing things. Even in touristic places like the temple of Karnak in Egypt where I lost myself in corners of the temple and saw some hieroglyphs that tourists never see, in Venice I found a corner that only Venetians go to, in Shanghai I had lunch in a hidden restaurant that only locals know, my wife and I got lost in the streets of Split in Croatia and Kinvarra in Ireland and found farmers' markets there... all these beautiful places and experiences we have had just because we have allowed ourselves to wander around. We have let the local people, streets, sounds, colors and smells open our senses and gently guide us.

People tend to believe that because the company is divided into departments, the one they are already in is the only one they can go through to climb the ladder. And by extrapolation, that the only way to go up on the ladder of hierarchy, is to go in a straight line.

With this exact mindset, I have found myself stagnate in my career growth because I was too stubborn to move across to another department or field. I had moved countless times from department to department, horizontally or slightly up, but I had never been that stubborn than at that time. I ended up staying there (in the same position) for 6 years with no promotion, and barely any pay-raises. I took it on myself to grow laterally by developing my skills, taking more responsibilities, enlarging my scope of influence and reach. I became so much more knowledgeable and capable than any of my counterparts in the company. At the same position than them, I had become an expert in my field and famous in the group. Until one day I gave up trying to climb the ladder straight up, and the opportunity presented itself for me to move across to another department, with even more learning opportunities. That was the time for my career to actually take a boost. Now, the opportunities that I created for myself in these 6 years of "stagnation" saved me from insanity and utter boredom as I used the time of comfort zone to expand laterally my scope of responsibilities and skills. Overall, I cannot even consider these 6 years as a waste of time, as I took it on myself to create these opportunities for (personal) growth. The point however, is that we need to break the prejudices and shift our paradigm of "straight-line-up-growth", more commonly called promotion. This is a good time to go back to read again the beautiful quote from Jim Rohn (Chapter 1 – Goal Setting).

"Once you stop learning, you start dying" – Einstein.

Curiosity has unfortunately started to disappear. The younger workforce, especially Millennials believe, more often than not, that they know – if not all – more than most. Their expectations are therefore disproportionate in the face of what companies and managers can offer, especially those from older generations and older schools of thought. Their motivation levels are coincidently affected by a lack of curiosity, as the information is readily at their fingertips. They do not need to "learn" anything really, they just need to know how to get the information. This lack of curiosity is also taking a toll on the innovation that they can bring to the company. Yes, they think differently, and this is a gold mine of innovative ideas for those of us curious enough to ask them for their input. But from my own experience, there is a harsh roadblock to that innovation speed-train once their list of ideas has been exhausted. And this is mainly due to a lack of curiosity.

You see, their point of view is that the world should revolve around Millennials, so the level of adaptability is quite low and the stress they feel is long and painfully lived. They have a sense of not fitting in, a feeling of always wanting more for them, and practice routinely and unconsciously the WIIFM (What's In It For Me) approach to decision making.

If you understand what they are going through, surely you do not want to be in their snickers now.

Have you ever considered that Millennials are not a generation, that they are not people, that "Millennials" is just a pattern of thoughts, a mindset? Unfortunately, we are all prone to that lack of motivation and that loss of curiosity.

There is a beautiful French song by Francis Cabrel that tells the story of two people who meet by bumping into each other; one was always looking at the ground, the other was always with the "nose" up in the sky. I say: look around.

Sure we are now climbing our mountain, but imagine all the beautiful things that we pass by without looking. We look but we do not see. Imagine all that our senses capture but that we do not pay attention to because *"We're on schedule"*, all that we could discover with a little bit of curiosity.

So keep looking, be curious, keep learning; *"I have no special talent, I am only a passionate curious"* – Einstein

CHAPTER 9.

ASK AROUND

THE ART AND SCIENCE OF ASKING QUESTIONS IS THE SOURCE OF ALL KNOWLEDGE
– THOMAS BERGER

DON'T BE SUCH A MACHO… TALK TO THE LOCALS… YOU MIGHT FIND SOMETHING QUITE SYNCHRONISTIC… FOR THERE IS ALWAYS SOMETHING NEW TO SEE, TO LEARN

Men have a certain reputation while travelling, never to ask for direction. Ladies, how often the man you spend most time with asks for direction, asks a shop attendant for the location of what he is looking for? Gents, how often do you ask for help? Ask the lady you spend most time with to answer this question about you and compare the two perceptions. Chances are, the answers are quite different.

At work, unless your job is currently in an office, in a deserted place, chances are that you have colleagues around.

Talk to them – and I mean talk, don't email or whatsapp them – you will gain much knowledge of what works and what doesn't. Although we live in a connected world, Claudia, who is so insightful, calls the Social Media Generation the "Generation Dis-connected". She put the finger right on it! Connect with people... face to face. Find yourself a mentor; someone who has the experience, a higher level than the one you are at now and who can guide you and suggest directions. Learn from others. I always like to say that workwise, the biggest lessons I have learnt are not about what to do, but about what not to do. Find yourself a coach too, not a cheerleader... I mean a real coach. This person is supposed to help you reach your goals, help you find resources that are available to you, help you find solutions that fit you best, who is here to offer you support on your path, but also to identify the self-limiting beliefs you have created for yourself and that slow you down on your path, and challenge the status quo that you protect so much.

In the chapter "Road Map" I shared my experience of completing the project in 10% the time that it took my classmates. There is another lesson there: I would not have been able to achieve this feat if it was not for my friends' mistakes. In other words; they helped me complete my project, and I would never had been able to do that alone.

I have read hundreds of books, watched videos, webinars and webcasts of leaders, thought leaders, CEOs, I read countless articles from business influencers, and they all say the same thing: *"If you think you can do everything alone... you're a fool and you will not succeed as easily as you potentially could"* and they all conclude the same: the number 1 (or 2 depending on who you ask) fault in leaders is not to ask for help. Well, this roots up from either a certain lack of humility or the presence of fear... from a lack of self-confidence.

Making decisions is part of everybody's daily life. We

make decisions for everything. Decisions about how we're going to do today, what time we're going to wake up, what kind of breakfast we're going to have, where to go for lunch and what to eat, decisions about if we should have a meeting or not about this, if we should attend a specific meeting or not, if it is worth engaging with a coworker or not, if we should say yes or no, or what to do when we are interrupted. We make decisions about making decisions. We make decisions all the time. Most people feel overwhelmed by this decision-making syndrome.

In order to ease our life and make it less stressful, you can reduce the amount of decisions you're making every today. You can first plan your next day ahead of time so that in the morning your clothes are all ready, your socks and ties sorted out, your breakfast bowl is ready, the cereal box next to it, your water kettle is full and ready for your coffee. You create a routine for minor things that you don't need to use your brain for in making decisions. You can just do it as a small practice, as a hobby for 3 main regular periods of your day. See for yourself how your mind relaxes already. You can also reduce the amount of decisions you make by asking people around for the help. This is not only about asking for assistance it is also about delegating what you don't need to do yourself and you overburden your mind with. You can ask your secretary for making some decisions, you can delegate to your subordinates as I empower mine to make day to day decisions on my behalf. What I just have to do then is only approve of the decision or not, just to maintain a minimum level of control. John Spence wrote in his brilliant book Awesomely Simple four types of decision-making that has been with me since I have read his book, and assists me tremendously every day to delegate or to make decisions myself.

Four decisions levels (John Spence):
Level 1: you own it completely; I hired you for this.

Level 2: get advice from the appropriate person, then you decide; you own it.

Level 3: the decision is a team decision however it is my responsibility; I own it.

Level 4: this is my decision, this is my responsibility I might ask for your input, but I am the decision maker.

An additional and very valuable tool in decision-making is to understand what kind of sorting patterns you apply. When we make decisions we prioritize our personal interests in the situation. So when we make a decision our brain is automatically sorting the importance, the relevance and interest that we have in that specific topic. People are either interested in: things, places, information, people or activities. This will transpire in the way we talk, the language we use, what our tone of the voice emphasizes on. If you ask yourself *"Why did I go to that place? Why did I do that? Why did I go for that activity rather than another? Why did I follow someone's decision rather than another? Why did I make that statement rather than another?"* You will notice that there is one of these five points of interest; things, places, information, people and activities that you are mostly excited about or attracted to. What aroused your interest? Did you go there because of the people you might meet there or that you knew were there (people)? Or, did you go because you were hoping to learn something new (information)? Or because of the things that you could do there (activities)? Or because of the location and the surrounding (place)? Or because of what is there (things)?

The language used by a person who is more people-oriented would be talking about the people they get to meet, the people who will be attending the networking event, the presentation, it would mention names, they will talk about what happened to some people, and that will transpire in relating what they liked about the event.

The person who is more interested in places will talk

about the environment, the location, where it is and how beautiful the place is, they will go in describing the surroundings, the atmosphere of the place etc.

A person primarily interested in sorting decisions based on activities will talk about what happens in that event, that location, what people do over there, what are the different options of things to do there. This person will make a speedy decision to go to that specific place because of something specific that can be done there.

The people who are primarily attracted to information will be interested in the knowledge that they can acquire, about the data and the information that is available to them. They will talk about new facts, information and data that they collected and that contributed to their decision to go.

The person who is primarily interested in objects and things will describe what is there in that location.

You see, telling your colleagues what you prefer and finding out what they prefer will make a big difference in your work relationships. For instance, I had a colleague who was talking so much, and taking me around in circles because he just wanted to spend time with people (people interest) while I am interested in "information". So he understood that irrelevant information is not working well for me and the relationship became much better. Because of my preference for information, I switch off very easily if the discussion is not bringing me "interesting". It is just a brain thing, there is nothing personal in this. See how important it is for me to tell this to my colleagues so that they don't freak out when I am quiet with them when they talk about random things? And I can make efforts especially in this field to make the connection. Some colleagues are primarily interested in activity, so they would go for outings together, regardless of who is coming or not, just for doing something themselves. Some misinterpret the invitation as something personal "he likes me" while that person will happily go with someone else if that person declines. It is therefore difficult for this person to do an activity in a group with others for the sake of being together. Take the example of a race as a team, if this person is faster, it will be very challenging for him to wait for his teammates because he is here for the action... not for the others. Again, there is nothing personal about it, and you see how important it is to get this clear for everyone in the team to make the work relationship better. Open up to others to make them know what you prefer, and be curious about what makes your colleagues tick. Just ask.

Asking questions is one critical skill that is lacking in a lot of leaders these days. They assume that they have to know everything and that they have to make all decisions. These are the micro managers, those who will breathe in your neck rather than utilizing the strength of the team members. Unfortunately this culture is so well spread out that it impacts every company's performances... negatively. The team members do not feel trusted, the subordinates do not feel involved and engaged.

Because of the myth that a good manager knows how to do everything that his subordinates are supposed to do, many managers and leaders end up creating the belief that they have to prove their worthiness and prove to the world that they are at the right place. This obviously, as you must have experienced yourself brings about a behavior from these managers that is overpowering, questioning, micromanaging. And maybe these people do not deserve to be where they are. But for most of them it is simply a question of low self-esteem and deep lack of self-confidence.

Realize that no matter what, your team members will know things differently. They are the ones doing the job. They are the ones in front of the clients, they are the ones facing the challenges, handling the complaints, or at least receiving them, from the horses' mouths, they are the ones who live inside the system. They are the ones directly affected by the processes, they are the ones who must "put a smile on the face", they are the ones who have to do what you are asking of them, and they see what works and what doesn't. Whether you like it or not, many a time, they know best.

Involve your team, your colleagues, engage them. You have many tools at your disposal to harvest the knowledge and ideas of your team members:
- Put them in groups/teams and give them projects, to answer a difficult question or to solve a challenge for your company
- Conduct brainstorming sessions with employees, ideally from different departments, different backgrounds, different levels in the organization, different decision making powers
- Drive design thinking sessions to help solve an issue or challenge that your company is facing
- Lead a Start/Stop exercise to ease and simplify processes, also great to solve issues
- Foster a lateral thinking session to find innovative ideas

Not all of us are made to be leaders. This is not to say that leaders are born, rather, that not all of us are interested into being a leader.

For very long time I was seeing my future as being only a number two in a company, simply because I was young and I was not extroverted enough to impose my decisions. I was very happy when I was involved and when I was asked for my opinions as well as requested for a mediating advice. But I was not ready at the time to imagine taking the responsibilities and the consequences of making the big decisions. On top of all, being a highly introverted person, it was absolutely unconceivable for me to be a leader. I became content with just the way things were.

Manager or Leader?

There's a great difference between being a manager and being a leader in the words of Peter Senge in the book called *The fifth discipline* Senge describes a manager as somebody who is working inside the system while a leader is somebody who is working on the system. A manager is by default somebody who is hands-on, at least on the people, not necessary on tasks alone, and focuses on the day-to-day operations. A leader is somebody who has a bird's eye view, who hopefully has a vision for the company or for his department, and who is able to guide, direct and give directions to his team because he sees where to go. We say *"Lead by example"*, not *"Manage by example"*. A manager is somebody who is going to tell people what to do. A leader is somebody who is going to be either at the front, on-the-floor or in the trenches, or be at the back supporting his team. The leader will have a point of view that is quite different from the manager's. In an extreme case the manager would be so hands-on that he would be actually just a subordinate, glorified. And on the other extreme of the spectrum the leader would be so high up in his ivory tower that he will be completely disconnected to the team. Ideally a subordinate would eventually move into a managerial position and the manager will grow into becoming a leader, because a manager needs to know what his team has to do so he can better control, direct and manage them. A leader does not necessarily need to be previously a manager. However the experience of working in lower levels of the organization is an addition to the toolbox of the leader who has been in their shoes before taking that charge, being a manager himself, because the leader would have in turn, managers under his wing. So it is easier for the leader to lead managers if he knows what the managers are supposed to do and have a view of the business that encompasses as many aspects of the organization as possible. But the leader does not have to go down to the level of the subordinate, handle every single detail of what that person is supposed to do. Should he go down to that level, he will surely lose his objectivity in regards to where the company and spend too much time that could be delegated to other managers. To take Newton's expression *"We are but dwarves sitting on the shoulders of giants"*. The Giants are the doers, the dwarves are but the leaders, for the Giant is the one who is walking and the dwarf is the one who can see much farther while totally dependent on his team.

First of all, you have to identify if you work better as the decision-maker or as an advisor. Then how do you work in the relationship at work: are you better as a supervisor and that means taking also the ownership and responsibilities of the decisions that are happening in your company whether you are the decision-maker or not, or are you better as a subordinate, or you better working with others as being part of the team, as a team member.

Once you have identified your work relationship as well as your input style, and you plug it into the matrix below, you will see the combination and how you more can work even more effectively.

Work relationship / Input matrix	Decision Maker	Advisor
Supervisor	1. You're the boss	4. Conflict
Team Member	2. Emerging leader	5. Advisor of the group
Subordinate	3. Conflict	6. Number 2 position

You will have noticed in this matrix that there is no Leader position. This is because I take "leadership" not to be a position, rather a mindset. The brilliant book by Robin Sharma *The leader with no title* will give great insights to anyone interested in taking their work and future in their own hands. A supervisor by default is a manager, but not necessarily a leader. If you are a supervisor through internal promotions and end up being the superior of your previous peers but work better as an adviser you might have a conflict of how you want to manage them now. There might be a conflict because if you're not confident with yourself to make decisions, then your supervisor will bypass you and will directly involve your team in the decision-making process. This is very good but there will be no leadership there; only management. Your team and your subordinates will be confused because you will involve them a little only because you are the advisor not them.

The supervisor who is also a decision-maker type is obviously the boss (1). This is a great combination, although at the risk of being a bit forceful. This is also the trait of a strong, sometimes regarded as being "tough", leader. Things might get easier on that person as time goes by, and if he or she involves the team; By getting information, getting opinions, involving the individuals and engaging the members into the process.

On the other hand, if the supervisor of an advisor type (4) then who is going to make the decisions? S/He will appear to be a person who is involving nobody and you will appear to be somebody who is "hands off" and do not want to get your hands dirty.

A team member who is of a decision-maker type is an emerging leader (2). As such he will be working alone quite successfully also because he's the one making the decisions anyway. When I say emerging leader that means that he has the tools, the position and the inclinations to making decisions that will build his credibility. As he makes decisions that are for the good of the group and the individuals of the group, people will start to follow him.

A team member who prefers to be an advisor (5) becomes an advisor to the group he is part of. Now this person, his/her role and impact will be highly dependent on working in a team. Such a person will very likely be successful working at all in a group, in a position that becomes critical to the projects given to the team.

A decision-maker type hold the position of a subordinate (3) will feel equally frustrated as in the position (4). This is what happened when I came out from my MBA. I got a mid-management position – not really subordinate but everybody have a boss. I had the tools and knowledge to make decisions but I could not get to my position as a decision-maker considering that my supervisor was really hands-on; I wanted to make all the decisions. So there was a conflict I want to be the decision-maker but I was under a boss who wanted to make the decisions himself. It happens also very often when, as a director or even higher levels in the organization, your direct boss is a micromanager. You have the frustration of having the rights and the opportunities to make the decisions however your direct supervisor is the one overruling your decisions. Also, the team will lose confidence in you or they will see that you have actually no power or at least, not that much. And that obviously will become a dread and a threat to your credibility and will of course reflect in the declining performance of your department.

And finally a subordinate who is an advisor would be an ideal number two in an organization (6). The person is not necessarily going to make the decisions. He is the influence, the man behind the curtain, he does not make the calls but with the confidence, the tools of strategy, he will have the security of being the advisor to his boss.

As part of a group trekking in our mountain together, it is very important to know what place in the group each have, and who the group leader is. As you can imagine, if everyone wants to be the decision maker, there will be no harmony in the group and disastrous results can happen.

This part is not only to guide you in what position is more adapted to your natural style (Decision-maker or Advisor) it is also for you to see which is more appropriate to the job position you are holding in the organization. In the light of the matrix shown above, you will have the indications of what tools, skills and resources you will need to acquire so that you can adapt your style to the requirements of the job in order to succeed in your position.

CHAPTER 10.

SHIT!

PEOPLE CHANGE, THINGS GO WRONG, SHIT HAPPENS BUT LIFE GOES ON
– OJ TAYLORT WAYNE ASSMAN

SHIT HAPPENS… GET OVER IT!

If you still believe that everything can happen according to your plan, either you are deluded, or you believe you are some lucky chap. Luck does count, but you have to be ready to face the music if troubles come your way. Do not go the other extreme of trying to dodge all the bullets, it might take way too much of your time and energy. Also, and maybe most importantly, trying to do so will take your attention away from what is really going on around you. I have seen so many people in this situation that they ended up being paranoid, believing that there was some conspiracy and plots put together against them. I'm sure you know someone like this: *"The-world-is-against-me"* type. This kind of approach to life will make you turn your back on doors of opportunity that present themselves to you and that could have offered you new, exciting and enriching experiences.

On a difficult mountain road, the mind becomes a very dangerous enemy. If you let any obstacle put you down, any twist of ankle get to your head, any dead end lose your temper, then you are in for a very long and disturbing ride on an emotional roller coaster. That is when even smaller difficulties will have negative impacts as powerful as the bigger ones. And then comes in the negative talks of: "*I cannot make it*", "*Why did I do this?*" "*I should not have…*", "*I cannot…*", "*I am not good enough*".

"*It's not about how often you fall, it's about how many times you get back up*", they say.

Flexibility and adaptation

Instead, what if you tried to imagine that everything that is happening to you was a conspiracy… for you to learn more, to experience something new, for you to grow and develop towards what you want and get you closer to what really matters to you?

When studying NLP, you learn what are called "presuppositions", that we suppose are true before anything else. These are like pre-determined, suggested guidelines to follow and that are foundations upon which the practitioner shapes a map of the world that is supportive of a successful and enjoyable life. One of them states that "every behavior has a positive outcome in some context". This means that any given way that someone acts, in a certain circumstance, certain context, certain situation, that behavior would be appropriate. I have found this point to be of much importance for me in my career as well as in my life. I no longer judge people, their attitudes, decisions or behavior so harshly, for I understand that they have their own personal reasons for doing so. I have realized that whatever happens is not necessarily bad; it is just that it is a matter of perspective. As the saying goes: the evil doer is the good doer from the other's side. Truth is in the eye of the beholder, although we might not always see it that way. So it occurred to me that I try to understand the other one's point of view, trying to really understand what could be the motivation for the person to behave in such a way. It does not mean that I am going to condone the action or necessarily agree with it, but it gives the perspective that my view of the situation is not everyone's. We share a common world although we see it through our own colored lenses… it is all a matter of perspective.

For instance our daughter, before even being 6, knew already what she wanted, and of course to our own exasperation what she didn't want, and she would not hesitate to share her opinion with us, directly in our faces. She refused to do what we asked of her if that was not aligned with her desires. In addition to this she was very shy, to the extent that she appeared to be "wild" and anti-social to people whom we introduced her to. As you can imagine, in some occasions this led to quite uncomfortable situations with what appeared to be embarrassing and bad behaviors. However, looking at it from the opposite perspective, we would be extremely happy if she was to display the same behavior to a stranger who would offer her candies in the street and ask her to follow him, wouldn't you? It is a matter of perspective and context.

Let's try to apply this to something that is closer to you. If you take the list of your "weaknesses" from the "tools" section, I would like you to take some time and ponder the following: these very same weaknesses could be actually very positive in some context… name at least one for each.

My Weaknesses	Context in which it would be positive

This might be quite a difficult exercise for some, however, once you manage to find a convincing context in which the weakness is no longer viewed as such, you realize even more the power of focusing on your strengths, don't you?

So many of us react before even understanding the situation or the person in front of us. I hear a lot of people I coach who are unhappy with the way others respond to them, the way others behave with them. This in turn creates expectations that the very same situation will be repeated in the future, it creates tension, and stress. This is what behavioral psychologists call *learned behavior*; the self-sustaining cycle, self-fulfilling prophecy that through conditioning, the results and their causes continuously repeat themselves. This in turn takes the form of angst, anxiety, apprehension, expectation, and eventually to the actual negative situation of meeting that specific person, the avoidance of what is perceived to be conflict or even the generation of fear of public speaking.

How different would your life be if you were to know what pushed or motivated that person to do what she did? What power would that give you in the turning of events? What opportunities would this give you in creating the change in relationships and situations that you wish to see with your colleagues and teams?

Feedback

"I have not failed, I have found 1,000 ways that did not work" – Thomas Edison

Another "presupposition" that is highly important for the management of our personal states and corresponding responses is: *"There is no such thing as failure, there is only feedback"*. What this points towards is two-fold: one is the cause-consequence effect, and two, that people's behaviors and reactions are just that: reactions. Of course there are a lot of factors that affect the other person before meeting you, but the reaction and evolution of the conversation with that person in front of you, at this very point of time will vary greatly based on your interaction with him/her at that time because every interaction is an exchange, which implies a two-way direction. Imagine one of your colleagues who is agitated with a report that has been criticized by someone else. The ways you address this person right now can either enervate him even more, keep him in the same state or appease him. There is already pre-established premises resulting from past events – prior to meeting you – so his reaction to your involvement has nothing personal to it; it is only a chain reaction. Furthermore, the evolution of the conversation you are having with that person, worsening, remaining the same or getting better is only a feedback to the way you interact with him at this time. Nothing else.

So instead of interpreting and taking it personally that he doesn't want to talk with you, that he maybe doesn't like you, or that he has something against you, just take the response as: *"The way I interacted with him/her did not yield the effect that I was looking for"*. This is the feedback about the interaction you just had with him – not about you as a person. Recall a similar situation that you went through recently, put yourself back into it and you say this sentence to yourself. How different do you feel? While detached from that situation, what feedback do you get now? Do you feel like *"I could have done it differently"*, *"I can try something else next time"*? Do you notice that you could have been better prepared for the discussion? Something else? Maybe you did not have a specific goal in approaching him/her and you were taken aback. And maybe the feedback is that it was just not the right time.

In *The 7 habits of highly effective people*, S. Covey makes a point to *"understand before being understood"*. The thing is that communication is a door that swings both ways, and what prevents it from swinging smoothly is clarity and feedback. How can you have a proper, clear and mutually understanding discussion if you do not even know what the person in front of you is trying to tell you, if you do not know what the other wants to express? Are you stubborn enough to relentlessly try to get your point across before anything? What are you trying to achieve?

Obviously some people will say: *"Well, s/he should not react like this, anyway"* And I reply: *"... And how do you react right now?"* Wouldn't you feel better if, when you have a bad day the person in front of you was aware, agile and flexible enough to adapt their reaction and speech to your mood? How about for that person to not take it personal when you lash at him/her for no personal apparent reason?

Well, now you have the awareness that it is not about you as a person, it is only about the way the communication goes, and with this feedback that the person is freely giving

you now, you can do something about it.
So yes indeed, shit happens... don't make it personal, get over it, adapt and just change your style.

CHAPTER 11.

CRISIS

A CRISIS IS A TERRIBLE THING TO WASTE
– D. Clark, CEO of Merck

EACH CRISIS IS A BLESSING IN DISGUISE, A DOOR OPENING TO NEW EXPERIENCES, AN OPPORTUNITY TO TRANSCEND YOURSELF AND THE WORLD

In difficult times, there are two general kinds of reactions attitudes; Optimism or Pessimism.

On a traitorous path in the mountain, as we have seen in the previous chapter, the way we see obstacles will impact our progress on our path. A negative mindset will have the better of you, and your life. If on our trek in the Annapurna we had been pessimistic about our capacity to finish the trip, to make it to the next house, what would have happened? What would have happened if one of us would have given up, sat down and insisted to stop to walk until someone would have come to pick us up? Who would have come in the middle of nowhere to take us to a nice, warm cozy hotel? With no mobile coverage, no internet, no electricity? Our mindset is what got us going.

Ask yourself; when I face an issue, do I tend to look at the worst case scenario, or do I look at the positive side of it? What kind of language, words or expressions do you use when you hear about a problem?

I am more of an optimist guy, so the sentence that I use most often when I hear a bad news, and it has become almost a natural reaction for me, is *"Well, at least..."* or *"Well, the good thing is..."*

How do you tend to react more often?

This is a question for you to be open and honest with yourself about so that you are aware of your default coping-mechanism. There are of course pro's and con's to either way; a pessimistic person will be looking at the negative side of the situation while at the same time also be sensitive to potential issues that one might encounter, making that person cautious and prevent issues from arising on the way. Conversely, an optimistic person will look at the bright side of the situation while actually also discarding the seriousness of it and not necessarily take adequate actions.

Once you are aware of what you revert to automatically, you will be able to take a step back and be more objective to the situation at hand and take the measures that are appropriate, in a balanced manner. Also, in a group, you might want to have a mix of individual that represent each type so that the meeting and the ideas coming out of it are well balanced for the most effective results.

In Chinese, the word crisis is written like this:

The first character on the left means "Danger"... but the second, on the right means "Opportunity". How interesting is that?

I strongly believe that millennia-old languages such as Chinese hold wisdom in their origins. And you will certainly agree that there is certainly some of it in these two characters where Crisis is the balance between the potential negative and potential positive – yin & yang both – which actually hides an opportunity. This is also the reason why I like to call myself, not optimistic which sounds too jolly now, but opportunistic. It does sound negative because of the pejorative meaning this term has been given, however, now that you have read about these Chinese crisis characters, you might want to consider the similar alternative.

Just last weekend, I heard again one of my friend talk about luck, and how lucky I was to find my current job. He told me: "there are 2 ways of getting a new job, especially one that you really enjoy: 1 is through connections, 2 is by luck". I could not disagree more! Boy-scouts swear by constant preparation and made it their motto "always prepared", and Lolly Daskal who wrote *The Leadership Gap*; adds to it the opportunistic approach that I have adopted for myself when she says that "*Luck is when preparation meets opportunity*". I love this sentence because it goes exactly in the direction of the wisdom of these Chinese characters.

So, what is "luck" for you? What is your definition of luck? Something that is given by some other source or something that you can impact, that you have some control over? This will give you a brief idea of how much control over your life you believe you have, and how much impact you believe you can have on your own success. Is Luck something that you do not yet understand or is it something that you create?

CHAPTER 12.

MISTAKES

A MISTAKE IS AN EVENT, THE FULL BENEFIT OF WHICH HAS NOT YET BEEN TURNED TO YOUR ADVANTAGE – EDWIN LAND

MISTAKES ARE IMPORTANT… THEY ARE WHAT MAKES YOU GROW

When my clients and the people I mentor or coach ask me what my biggest lessons have been, I like to answer: *"My greatest lessons where not about what to do, but about what not to do"*. This comes from a place where I have learnt – through a very long process I admit – to accept my mistakes as part of a learning process. You may tell an employee what not to do and he will still do it. But letting him learn by doing, which by the way is a common expectation the millennials have of their managers, and giving him the space to fall, this is where you show respect to the individuality of the person and you have the opportunity to teach and coach on the take-away. Mistakes are an essential part of our learning process as humans. They teach us in a more effective way. There is a memory that is built from what one does.

There is an old saying; *"A fool learns from his mistakes, a wise man learns from others'."*

When you make a mistake, provided that you admit even later that you are responsible, how do you tend to react? Do you blame others? Or even yourself? Do you try to appease everyone by promising that everything will be fixed and prevent them from being angry with you? Do you distract people by changing the conversation to drive away the attention from your mistake? Are you remaining super cool (on the outside) by rationalizing and minimizing the importance of its consequences? Do you react at all? Virginia Satir explains the 5 different characters and types of response to stress in her great book *Your many faces*:

A "Blamer", as the name points out, is one who does not take the responsibility of the issue, or blames himself. An important note to make I believe is that in the case of self-blame, one part of the self is literally not accepting the responsibility and blames it on another part of the same self. The positive side of this modus is that it is important sometimes to tell your team or an individual that they screwed up, and that if they want to take ownership, they have to take the consequences too. The negative side of this attitude is that it will easily be taken to show no support, involvement or responsibility in the situation.

A "Placater" is someone who tends to please, pacify or make concessions in order to smooth things out. The basic principle of this approach is to avoid conflict, escalation, anger or damage to one's reputation. The positive side of this stance is that it appears to presents an "understanding" attitude towards the other. The negative side shows a non-decisive take on the situation, and although it might appear to take some responsibility for what has happened, the person in fact does not take ownership for her decision or point of view which very often is seen as being weak.

A "Distractor" will attempt to change the conversation, he might say something that does not even make sense or not be relevant to the conversation. The basis of this approach could be summed up with the saying: "If you can't convince them, confuse them". The positive side of the distractors is that they will assist in lifting the grave mood of the situation, especially when others take so many things so seriously. The negative side of this attitude is the obvious refusal to face the situation and therefore will very likely not look or find solutions. A person taking this approach also does not taking either responsibility or ownership of the situation and is very unlikely to help out.

A "Computer". Computing means that the person is not showing any signs of emotions, he is very rational about the situation and will deal with facts mainly. It is however important to specify that it does not automatically imply that this person does not feel any emotions at all. Quite the contrary, underneath the very calm surface, a storm might be raging, but not a ripple will be left to be seen. The person is (appears to be) quite detached from the situation. The positive side of this stance is that the person will remain "professional". Unfortunately, the negative side of this response will display a cold non-reactive, almost psychopathic, attitude to some extent which will very easily be perceived to be care-less.

A "Leveler" is someone who responds congruently to the situation wherein the words & body language match the feelings expressed. This person can be reasoned with and a healthy discussion can take place in order to correct the issue or prevent it from occurring again in the future. The good thing about this reaction is that "you get what you see"... no surprises, nothing hidden. Although it is the reaction that brings about a much preferred adult-like response, some people like to look at the negative in all things, so even this reaction might be perceived in this light.

For instance if the person shows emotions about the negative results of the situation, some might take it as being "emotional" or if he remains thoughtful about the results and not show "enough" emotions, the person will be perceived to be non-caring, and further be translated that as being "unprofessional".

You must be used by now; Find out for yourself, honestly, what kind of behavior you tend to display the most naturally, almost by habit, when faced with a difficult situation:

You have delivered a report that compiled a lot of information and that you have gathered through several sources. The report presents several obvious mistakes and your boss criticized the fact that you have not spotted them earlier before presenting it. How are you likely to react? Which of the above default characters do you display?

_____

_____

You have received a customer complaint that points out on the deficiency of a process that is currently in place, how do you respond to the guest? Which of the above default characters do you display?

_____

_____

A peer is criticizing the attitude of one or more of your subordinates, what are you likely to say? Which of the above default characters do you display?

_____

_____

Each of these behaviors and reactions present both positive and negative parts, depending of course on the perception of who is judging. It is indeed about perception, but also about how we want to interpret situations and behavior. It is however clear that some of them are more effective to recover from mistakes than others and are more likely to yield positive results and solutions. It is also great to know that, although these are highly engrained and natural reactions, they can be changed to a more effective and appropriate one to fit the desired outcome.

The bottom line really is that if you focus on the issue, then you will have negative emotions and attitude. It will be very difficult to find a solution to it. If you focus on the solution, then the attitude is a lot more positive and the emotions will be very different.

Back on the mountain, I have been facing a very large crack on the side of the mountain that was scary to cross. Did I have a negative attitude towards it, thinking that it is too big to cross, that it is too deep and that if I fall I would die? Did I keep on repeating to myself *"This is a huge jump to make"*, focusing on the problem? No, I focused on finding a solution, and I focused on the different options that I had, eventually I found my way to go to the other side successfully without falling or hurting myself at the reception.

Here are some powerful questions that will help you – feel free to put down your answers below:
What prevents me from achieving what I want?

What is the worst thing that can happen if I did it anyway?

What's the worst thing that can happen if I didn't do it?

What am I going to do next?

CHAPTER 13.

STEPS

I HAVE ARRIVED. I AM HOME. MY DESTINATION IS IN EACH STEP
– THICH NHAT HANH

THE PATH IS MADE OF STEPS… EACH IS AN EXPERIENCE, A WORLD OF ITS OWN… ENJOY THEM ALL!

So many people I have coached at work just want to be "there". I ask: *"Then what?"* … well, that's it; no answer. This is simply because these people mistake the tree for the forest. They believe that all is good at the top but they do not realize that what makes the person at the top be good (or bad) is the path that s/he has walked… and the learnings acquired on the way. Some will say: *"I have suffered, it took this amount of years to get where I am, my bosses have been tough with me and this is how I have learnt, and so should you"* … or: *"So will you"*. Sounds familiar? Unfortunately, this is because they mix the difference between knowledge and skills. Knowledge – through experience – will take time to acquire. They say *"Been there, done that"* as an accomplishment, however the big question is about what is done with this "knowledge"?

Skills are acquired, learnt, experienced. And if we consider that to be a leader is a combination of skills, character and attitude, then one does not have to be on top to be a leader. Countless books have been written about the qualities that the best leaders display. Do you really believe that these qualities appear by magic overnight once you are promoted as the boss? No, they are grown, brewed along the path that is walked to the top.

Learning is an attitude that I mention a lot at work. A beautiful quote posted by Collective Evolution says: *"If you are not willing to learn, no one can help you. If you are determined to learn, no one can stop you"*. Learning does not happen as a download of information (knowledge) but as a learning process, practice and sharpening and maybe even teaching.

As Confucius put it:
"Tell me and I will forget,
Show me and I might remember,
Involve me and I will understand."

And a Chinese proverb also says:
"The teacher learns as much as the student."

Learning is the corner stone of our growth as *human becoming*; it is the process that opens doors of opportunities along the way to creating the future that we want for ourselves and for our lives.

There are those who are more concerned about the big picture which allow them to see what others do not; they are the seers, the observers, the visionaries, they sit on the shoulders of giants and see trends and patterns. And there are those who are more concerned about the tasks, the details, which is great because without these people, nothing would get done. Any extreme would be counter-productive for one would become a passive contemplator (no action) and the other would become overly interested in the nitty-gritty and lose focus on the direction (no vision). The trick is to be able to balance both approaches: look at the big picture then, understand what needs to be done (tasks).

Option or Procedure?

If I asked you "*Why did you make this choice* (chose a decision of importance that you recently made)*?*" your answer will give you an idea of how, the process, you adopt before making up your mind and acting. There typically are two trends of "strategies" that people adopt: "procedures" or "options".

A person who is more inclined towards "Procedures" will be more likely to take a logical approach from the current situation and will see very little options available to her. It is a very linear way of looking at things, from past to present. Additionally, this person will prefer to be guided through tasks or a project. This person will also very likely have a to-do list of things to be done during the day. This approach can be very effective in order to achieve a goal that is clear for the next logical step is evident. As her manager, it is not recommended to give free range or carte blanche to this person, for she will be confused as to what to do next. Instead, just break down the path how you see it best, give some mile-stones and key points to go through. The more details, the better for this person.

A person who prefers options will be enjoying the "freedom" of doing things their way, in a non-linear fashion. Indeed this person is very likely to be more impulsive, but can also be procrastinating, but once she comes at a cross road, she will also take the time to weigh the pros & cons, look at the possible consequences of each possibilities. To give such an employee a check list and step-by-step of the project will make her feel suffocated. It is for the manager to learn how to delegate with trust (and follow up and check in on her). If you or your employee is primarily "optional", you just have to pay attention to not falling in the trap of wandering around and not accomplish much.

A person who enjoys procedures will have more opportunities to be highly focused on what is at hand. It is therefore slightly easier for this person to be present. An options-oriented mind does not prevent you from being present, but it is just more difficult because this mind just likes to wander around. It is again in the balance; one just needs a flexible mind that is able to shift from "Options" to "Procedures" in order to improve effectiveness, to be more rounded while at the same time remain present and mindful.

Mindfulness represents the capacity to be aware of ones' present state; physical, emotional and mental. *Mindfullness* is not digital, it is not that "either you are or you are not"; it is a spectrum that ranges from total *Anosognosia* and oblivion to being an absolute "empath". Physically, the more mindful one is, the more sensitive you are to feel what your body feels inside. Emotionally, the more mindful one is, the more you will be able to feel, locate and name the emotions that you are going through. You will even be aware of the feeling that precedes the emotion. Mentally, the more mindful one is, the more clearly your thoughts will be. You will be aware of the thoughts that go through your head, you will be able to remain aloof and just watch them, without having to unconsciously react to them. In addition to ones' awareness, mindfulness opens to environment and social awareness. Environmentally, the more mindful you are, the more sensitive (not necessarily sensible) you will be to any changes in your environment perceived by your 5 senses; temperature, smells, surfaces... Socially, the more mindful you are, the more empathetic you will be to a person's feelings and emotional state. A lot has been talked and written about Emotional Intelligence, while Empathy is nothing more than a higher level of mindfulness. It seems therefore counter-intuitive to ask people to increase their Empathy without talking about mindfulness first.

Dr. Jon Kabat-Zinn writes a lot about the positive clinical effects mindfulness brings to patients and how it assists in speeding up the recovery process. His fantastic book *Coming to our senses* shows not only the benefits of practicing mindfulness, it also covers the applications, even medical that mindfulness has on health and his patients. Personally, the way I have developed mindfulness over the years was by walking my way through from the more gross to the more subtle senses, starting off with touch; I developed by sensitivity by touching as many different surfaces, fabrics and material as possible. This sensitized my finger-tips. Then touching my own hands and arms. To sensitize my skin. Turning my attention internally, I meditated for a very long time until I became aware of my thoughts. Then, going down from my head to the chest, I became aware of my emotions, and eventually down to my guts, aware of my feelings. It has been a long process, and I am very proud of what I have accomplished because it has helped me know and understand myself and therefore learn a great deal about others – since we are not that different after all.

How is your time?

If I asked you to visualize a couple of events of your past, spaced enough from one another, say one event that occurred yesterday, one last week, and one a month ago, so that you can draw a "line" that links them all. What would that line look like? What direction would it take geographically around you, from the most recent to the more distant past? Now, if I asked you to visualize what you can imagine to happen tomorrow, a week from now, a month from now. And if you were to link all these events by another line. What would that line look like around you? What direction would it take, from the most recent to the more distant future? How do these two lines, past and future, connect? Do they connect inside of you or do they connect in front of you? This point of connection is your present. Where is it located? In front of you, on the side, high, low… or are you your present?

Some people have a timeline that is quite linear, in a sequence, you know; past, present, future – whether it goes from left to right, right to left, from up down or from down up – and the present is most of the time in front of them. This person is quite detached from events, is by-the-book, and enjoys timeframes, deadlines. This person sees things happen in front of their eyes. This employee will be likely to finish tasks on time, but not necessarily take things very personal, to heart, in the sense that they do it because it is business.

Some people have a timeline that is not quite clear. They sort events past and future in a random fashion and the Now is ever-present. This person who is part of their present, all around them, they enjoy options, see possibilities and a quite creative (or dis-ordered) in their choices and selection of memories. This employee will be very good at taking projects with not many guidelines, and because they are in the present, they will most likely take things to heart. They will be the craft-men of their work and will probably take criticism about their output personal.

It is my experience that either style has actually the opportunity to be present in whatever people endeavor at the time. The first person can slow down and look intently at the task at hand, zoom in, dive into the detail and enjoy this very moment. The second person is already thinking in slow-motion, so to speak, but with the view of many opportunities at once, past and future, has the capacity to relax their gaze to this moment alone and enjoy what is already around.

I have a mantra that I created for myself and that helps me tremendously in becoming more present: "This is the most important thing in the world". "This" actually stands for anything that I do, say or hear at the time. Anything, anywhere, anyone that is here is therefore the most important thing in the world at that time. I am definitely not present 100% of the time, but whenever I remember to do this, it brings me focus and full attention to what is now. I invite you to try it out and let me know how it goes for you.

In his fabulous book *The Prince*, Niccolo Machiavelli wrote that "*Someone raises himself to being a prince through some really wicked conduct*" which later got distorted and became the famous, yet wrongly attributed to him: "*The end justifies the means*". Nothing really supports the idea that Machiavelli ever really saw this as a "right" way, but it is a widely spread philosophy now, especially in the corporate world. Maybe it is just an excuse created for some to justify their acts. Nevertheless, I really like to use this idiom and to put it upside down and say: "*The means justify the ends*": The way, the manner, the state of mind you have on your path towards your goal will determine you reaching it or not. More importantly, the way things are done will determine the quality of the result.

The very common philosophical yet rhetorical question that follows then is: Is it more important for you to do things right or to do the right thing?

CHAPTER 14.

CHANGE

EVERYTHING CHANGES, CHANGE IS THE ONLY CONSTANT
– BASHAR

CHANGE IS THE VERY NATURE OF THINGS...
EMBRACE IT!

Do you need it or do you want it?
Let's dig in straight away and put ourselves in the situation; consider your current job, or the last job you had, and the conditions in which you chose it. What were the reasons for your choice? What is your true and honest answer to that? Did you make that choice because you had to; it was a need? Because you wanted to? Or because you could; you had the option? As you read these different views, you already see and get the feelings and emotions attached to the memory of your choice. From a very constrictive position of necessity (very much likely to

appear to be a no-choice stance) to an energetic, almost aggressive "wanting" approach to get it, which still brings more choice to the table. But when you look at this from an "Opportunistic" view – not the negative aspect of the word as we discussed it in previous a chapter – having the perspective to see that this choice is an opportunity for growth, development, to get closer to your goal, then the thrusting power behind this outlook is so much stronger.

When you come to a fork on the road, take it – Yogi Berra

One of the General Managers I worked with and from whom I learnt a lot from once said to our Employee General meeting, paraphrasing what a leader in the Middle East had said before him: "*If you do not change, you will be changed*". Now, with his *happy-trigger* reputation for letting people go quite fast, this statement brought quite a glacial feeling in the room and hairs raising on people's spines as you can imagine, but I believe it did not quite come out the way it was intended. However, when you take into consideration the language barrier, he meant to say that, even if you do not change, you will be forced to change, by the power of the circumstances.

Now, I always tell my team and employees who are either afraid of change (usually stemming from a fear of the unknown) or to those who do not want to change (very often because they are couched in their comfort zone) that what they need is "control". Control of their environment, control of the circumstances. Of course we know fairly well that there is so much that one can control. So the best way to ride the wave of change is actually to create it! If you create the change yourself, if you instigate it, they power is in your hands... you are in charge. Once this is the case, then there is nothing to fear. I was reading a recent on *Entrepreneur.com* that was talking about following trends (change). Kimanzi Constable concludes that "*If you're jumping from trend to trend, you might want to sit down and get clear about what your values are and what kind of business would match those values"*. This is precisely the point. Get your values straight, figure out your "Why" as Simon Sinek so eloquently puts it in his great book Start with why , then build your brand (business or personal) around them. Finally, do not budge; the niche, the clients, the audience, those who are ready for your message, ready for you, will be there. Everything moves, change is difficult because change is imposed upon you. Embrace change, be with what is. Create the change so it is not imposed on you.

CHAPTER 15.

CHANGE OF MIND

ONLY FOOLS DO NOT CHANGE THEIR MINDS
– FRENCH SAYING

IT'S ALRIGHT TO CHANGE YOUR MIND… THE JOURNEY IS WHAT'S IMPORTANT… SO EVERYTHING IS GOOD!

On the mountain, the worst attitude that one can have is to be arrogant about it. You are never "too ready" for it. Believing that you know it all, that you have done this before, that you are "too good" have killed thousands on the way. The same mountain path can be quite different from one hour to the next. The mountain lives and breathes; the terrain changes, rocks fall, trees fall, water runs, new streams appears, humidity, dryness, temperature changes make everything absolutely different. It is good to change your mind on the way and take a different path. What you need most is an open and flexible mind. I have been "caught" with my boy scouts patrol in a pouring rain that suddenly fell on us. We thought of taking a shortcut through the woods in the mountain, going down back to camp. We were 3 teenagers in charge of 4 much younger lads. The slope was about 60 degree angle and the floor got muddy in minutes. We were holding on to the vertical trees and every step could have been the last. After 15 minutes of very slow decent, we were all soaked, muddy, with chills of cold and fear, some of our scouts started to cry, one was shouting that we're going to die and my mind started to get convinced. Our "number 2" went further down to see what was ahead (down) of us and came back much later to inform us that there was a 5 meter cliff that very few of us could jump. Our leader decided to stay together and we turned back up again, slowly and surely, helping our younger friends to get safe. We changed our mind in order to guarantee our safety. We all arrived back to camp about 2 hours later, soaking wet, but safe and sound.

What really prevents people to change their minds is either stubbornness or a strong deep-rooted belief (which in turn translates in stubbornness). Whether one thinks that they know everything, or that they cannot learn from others, from any situation, or from some people only, then they do not grow. I am particularly fond of the quote attributed to Einstein: *"When you stop learning, you are dead"*. And how do you learn if you are adamant on your positions and opinions? I am not advocating a non-opinion stance; I am suggesting that having strong opinions sometimes more than never prevents you from learning. To have a strong opinion means that you know everything about the topic and therefore there is nothing left to add; your cup is full.

A non-opinionated person is very often prejudiced to be weak-minded for they do not have a strong stance on certain topics. And to an extent some see this as being so detached about certain matters that they appear to be careless. But a person who does have opinions but is aware that they are not set in stone, that they are based only on what is known to them, that they are not all knowing, that they have flaws, that person is ready to accept and is therefore more likely to grown & develop. What I see is missing more and more often is a sense of curiosity, a taste for exploration and a thirst for discovery. Curiosity has been labelled as being bad, perhaps as yet another way to control others: "(slap on the hand) *That's not your business*". Or is it? We do not have an issue of empathy, we have an issue of *curiosity*. Where is the interest about what others are going through? About what they have learned through their hurdles? Where is the curiosity of discovering and understanding others? To learn from them, Where did the wisdom of age gone?

Now people are more interested in knowing how many others "like" their opinion or agree with them in number of "thumbs up" without paying attention for a second to what the others have to say. People are very happy to throw in their 5-cent opinions about anything, just as long as they have any opinion about anything. It is as if we were all born with an opinion and it is about who shouts it the louder to the world.

Are you conscious or on auto-pilot drive?

Our level of "consciousness" is proportionate to our level of self-awareness. "Know thyself" was written on top of the temple of Delphi. Many managers and so-called leaders just hide their low self-confidence or their close-to-no-self-esteem feelings behind either a strong hand, oppressing or highly micro-managing at one extreme or by hiding behind a hands-off approach on the other end.

The first ones would not change their minds because they would (try to) control everything. It is therefore better for their subordinates to take a knee and take their words as Gospel. For them, there is no need to change their minds. Changing it would reveal some flaws in their decision making and unveil some vulnerability. How many times have you seen a superior refusing to admit that the very person they had hired (bypassing the red tapes) is not fit for the job? And how many times have you seen that anyone attacking that person is facing great danger? The micromanager lacks faith and trust towards their teams, but also towards themselves. The result is that they are so engrossed in the details and in the tasks that they do not have any vision, and end up contradicting themselves. It is not that they change their minds, it is just that they do not have any directions.

On the other side of the spectrum, those who are totally hands off do not have to (or do not want to) make any decisions. They are so not involved in the decisions that they do not have to make up their minds... or change their minds either. They believe that they appear to be consistent and magnanimous in their giving the opportunity for their team members to make the decisions. Unfortunately, when their team members ask for really help, they will refrain from getting involved, hands on which threatens the results greatly.

The other side of the curiosity coin that is lacking is vulnerability; allowing others to look into our "business" might reveal our phoniness, our weaknesses, our "not-so-knowing-after-all-ness". To change one's mind takes actually guts and self-esteem. It takes self-confidence to admit that we do not know it all. It shows vulnerability and the courage to face them. Unfortunately, you may know of some people around who have been promoted or have got a job that their experience or attitude does not justify. Coupled with a low self-confidence and you have the recipe for an aggressive person at work. That person feels the need to prove himself to others, at all cost sometimes, they lose perspective and become easily extreme in their approach with others.

The mind has the unfortunate habit to jump from one

extreme to the other. So a micro-manager who finally realizes the negativity of his management style will very likely jump to become hands-off, and vice versa. The team will for sure feel like they "traded the Devil for his mother". After a while, however, provided that there is enough awareness and willingness to learn, develop and grow, one can expect to see a stabilization of the management style with eventually a more balanced approach.

Einstein is famous for saying that *"The greatest absurdity is to continue doing what you have always been doing and to expect a different result"*.

So, don't hesitate to change your mind…set.

This again, takes courage, to get out of the vicious circle, to exit the cycle, to walk the path that is not the easier one to take. The only question that remains is: What do you want to achieve?

CONCLUSION.

*WE SHALL NOT CEASE FROM EXPLORATION
AND THE END OF ALL OUR EXPLORING
WILL BE TO ARRIVE WHERE WE STARTED
AND KNOW THE PLACE FOR THE FIRST TIME
– T.S. ELIOT, FOUR QUARTETS*

Throughout this book you have come to notice that being strategic at work starts with yourself and it follows very closely with how we interact with others. And with that I add: to be strategic is an attitude.

Imagine for a second that whatever you endeavor to accomplish would involve (almost) zero conflict. What would your path look like? Smoother, faster, easier… boring maybe? Conflict resolution is not necessarily about situations where people fight, it is about any time that there is disagreement about a common topic or point. This is actually an opportunity to learn about each other, about different views, it is about your grow and develop. It took me a long time to get this as I was trying to please everyone around me, avoid any altercation and bend at any comment. I came to realize that you cannot please everyone… take it from me; I'm French. As Churchill said: *"You've got enemies? Good, that means that you stand for something"*. Surely one the most common reason for projects to stop mid-way, for ideas not to be implemented, for strategies not to be executed to the end is actually because people involved have differences of opinions, have their egos not kept in check, have different agendas…. Basically because there is conflict.

The way I have been dealing with conflict for many years is simply by following the very simple idea that I coin: to "*PUT things in perspective*". And PUT, here stands for:
- Pause
- Understand
- Transcend

Pause

First things first: as soon as you see, hear or feel that there is a barrier in the communication or that your point is not clear to the person in front of you; pause! Especially if you have a short fuse, take a deep breath. Do not react. Just stop. Most of the arguments would be defused if this very simple step was taken from the very beginning of the conversation. As soon as the tension comes, the blood flow in your body increases, it goes to the extremities that need it the most to serve your body's natural response; to your legs in order to run away or to your hands in order to fight. Then the nervous system tenses, then the muscles. The tension builds in and because energy has been piling up, it needs to exit in a way or another; either vocally – raising of the voice, or even shout – or physically – an increase in the rhythm of your breathing, or more hand movement… until. Keeping one's head cool is of great importance in a work environment, for obvious reasons, but also because it projects an image that is not necessarily reflective of who you are, and, as importantly, it prevents you from being the most effective in resolving issues in the most efficient manner.

Understand

Understanding where the person is coming from at an intellectual level is a great way to take a step out of the situation and address the issue at hand effectively. However, to be empathetic, which means to put yourself in the shoes of the other person will bring about yet a different understanding of the person's point of view. This is a very commonly used expression that has yet to be explained in practical terms. Ready for one more exercise?

Take the example of a conflict or argument you recently had with someone. Re-live the event with as much detail as you can; what you saw at the time, what you heard around, the person talking... Imagine for a moment that <u>you are that person</u>. You may want to move around in the room to physically stand where you see that person. Imagine that you merge with that person and that you are inside that person's skin. And see in your mind's eye what that person would see. You then will see yourself from the other person's eyes. Now, imagine what that person was thinking at that time. Finally, imagine what that person was feeling... and feel it yourself.

This little exercise will make you see, literally, the situation <u>from that person's point of view</u> and feel what s/he felt at that time. This is empathy. Just to close the circle; imagine you come out of that person's body, change your location and move back to re-integrate yours. See, feel how different the person and the entire situation changes now.

Transcend

The above exercise helps you see things from a 1st position (yours) as well as from a 2nd position (the other person's). Now, imagine that you are outside the situation, not you and not the other. This is called the 3rd position. If you consider that the interaction between a person and another is a system in itself, the 3rd position places you outside that system.

From this location, what do you see, what do you here, what do you feel about the way the interaction is going? What new do you learn from that point of view?

Now, go back to the 1st position and bring in with you all the learning, experience and insights that you have had during this exercise, and the previous one.

How different do you perceive the situation now? How different to you see the person in front of you? How different do you see yourself within that situation now? How could you have dealt with the situation differently so that it would have been conducive to a different, more beneficial result for both parties?

Well, imagine that the whole situation occurred in this manner instead. Imagine that you say and do what you would have preferred to say and do at that moment. And let the situation unfold with a different turn of events. Imagine how the interaction is changing and evolving into something a lot more pleasant. Imagine how this changes everything and all the future events of all the parties involved. And fast forward all the future encounters and interactions with this person(s) after this one until you reach the present moment.

How different do you feel now? How different do you see that person now? What do you feel like telling that person? How much better and much lighter to you feel?

Once you understand fully, deeply, viscerally, then you transcend. Transcending goes beyond understanding. It is the realization that both parties have a common goal, and knowing what that goal is. In any conflict each party has its own agenda, its own outcome that one wants to reach eventually. This is why conflicts arise, because of the apparent difference in the agendas of the parties involved. Once you understand what the other side want of you, where the person is coming from, this is the time when you completely and fully integrate the other person's position. Transcending happens once you realize what the highest criteria or deepest reason for that person to hold his position is, what it is that that person wants to achieve. When you go back in the first position, bring to mind your personal highest criterion here; what are you trying to achieve in this situation? What are you reasons for standing your ground? What are you defending? What is it that you cherish so much that you go into arguing with another person about it? What is it that you truly want out of this conversation or situation? Once you reach a clear understanding of your own criteria, your own deepest reasons, this is where you will realize that there is a correlation, if not a merge of your outcome and that of the other person. This is transcendence.

The ability to perceive or think differently is more important than the knowledge gained – David Bohm

Throughout this book you have hopefully learned a lot more about yourself as well as about others, and everything in between. It is currently what is trending up as known as emotional intelligence. What really that is, is about getting a certain understanding of people. And for any of you of who have gone through emotional intelligence training or even read some material about it, you will realize that all these tools that I have given out actually encompass most of emotional intelligence material. These tools to some extend even go beyond emotional intelligence (EQ), whereby EQ itself is but a small part of the story.

What I wanted to achieve with this book is to help and assist you in designing a strategy for yourself in a work environment by showing you the seven steps that I have put in place from my varied experiences and knowledge of different psychological streams of thought that can be easily applied. I do hope that you have come out at the end of this book if not as a totally different person, at least as one more aware that there are tolls and resources available to you, and that are now at your fingertips for you to apply today. It is highly recommended that you go back to the book from time to time, pick a topic, a chapter, an exercise, re-evaluate yourself, re-evaluate your goals, audit and analyze your current style and adapt your strategies accordingly so that you constantly grow and develop. We all evolve and grow weather we want it or not. The question really is: *"Do I want to take charge of my life? Do I want to identify the most effective way of learning for me? Do I want to better my interactions with others so that I can reach my personal goals and outcomes that I've set out for myself to be the most productive, effective and efficient way?"*

The 7 steps give a progressive and clear framework to follow:
1. Goal setting
2. Where am I?
3. Road map
4. Tools
5. First step
6. Forget
7. Enjoyment

Although this book presents many insights, it offers you a perspectives of the events, people and of yourself. You have now this understanding at multiple levels and a clearer view of the complex beings that we are. All of these are made available to you now, they are easy to refer to, easy to dig in and to apply for your own life. I guarantee that from my own experience with myself and with the numerous people I have trained and coached, that these insights will help you get the success you want. I hope this book is going to be with you at home, at work, anywhere where you can always revert back & fallback, to should you need to assess, understand, and shed some light on the situation that you are facing at the time. Share it with those around you. Unfortunately these tools are not taught at school. However I strongly believe that it is never too late to learn them and to benefit from them to the best of your capacity. I often go back to the different material (any formats) that I have learned from and that I bookmarked for easy reference, I go back very often to the notes of the learnings I have acquired throughout my experience. Because I believe that by going through the material again, the additional experience I have acquired brings about new understanding, a new perspective, new insights that I learn even more. Haven't you watched a movie the second time and found out new things that you had not noticed the first time? Have you never experienced learning new things from the book once you had read it a second time? Kaizen, "constant improvement" in Japanese (usually attributed to companies... again) is the approach to business that has been followed by many highly successful 500 fortune companies that focuses on the company's results against that which I coined and promote *Jichigakuzen* (the constant study of oneself for ones' own personal development). This is a lot more personal, targeted at the individual themselves. Because I believe that each company is made by people, is made of people, and it is the individuals in the company that make the business succeed or fail. Although we are still in an era where companies are largely built in silo systems, it is up to the individuals within it and who want to achieve what they set out for themselves to reach, to change themselves, to learn more, to improve themselves, to constantly self-developed, that will allow them to reach their own joy and fulfilment. This is where I suggest employees themselves to take a strategic approach to take in the business world, which include how to set effective goals, to be clear about what one wants, understanding where we are and what path it is that we need to engage in, getting the tools that one will need on this road, biting procrastination and get started, relaxing on the path to maximize the opportunities that present themselves and finally, have fun. Keeping our egos in check along the way is one thing, and we just need to realize that our individual egos and our personal agendas hinder not only the companies but also ourselves to grow and eventually prevent us from reaching our full potential. It slows us down, making us linger in petty fights and distracting us from what really matters. Think back of a time when you had an argument with someone. Remember what your outcome was at the time. What drove you to go into that argument, and what made you stay in that argument? What made you hold your grounds? Looking back, how successful were you in reaching that outcome? Even more so, what did you gain from that, really? And also even more importantly what did you lose by going into that argument? What did you compromise? Was that argument really necessary? Was the learning experience strong enough for you to be willing to repeat that even again? Or would you rather go back in time and change the event because you realize that you could have handled it differently, reached your on outcome, and would not have lost what you have lost. Think back. Was your intention selfless or was it a "natural" automatic response? Was it for the benefit of the other person? Was it beneficial for the company? For the team? Or was it purely ego driven? Was it all only for your own benefit? These are the kinds of questions that I asked myself countless times and that made me realize that I did not have enough tools in order to reach my own goals. I had a goal that was relatively clear, however the path ahead of me was not, simply because I didn't have the tools to go through the path of life and that were presented here for you. So I took it upon myself to look for them, acquire and apply them so that I could reach my goals. And I am absolutely thankful and feeling blessed that I have had the opportunity to learn these tools... a little bit late, though, but looking ahead, I believe that it is never too late. These are now the tools that Claudia and I are teaching our daughter in order to prepare her for life, equipping her with a toolbox that we place in her school bag and that will give her such a head start. She will be clear with her goals, she will have a strategic way of living her life and a flexible approach to how she wants to walk her own path, even at work. Wouldn't you want your children to have the same benefits? I guarantee you that if applied, these tools will help you as much as they have helped me in my carrier. Then pay it forward; pass this knowledge onto others whether they are your colleagues, your subordinates, your family, your relatives... By teaching these tools to others, you will cement your knowledge, and this will in turn benefit not only you but your teams and for your company at large. You must also have realized that these tools are centered on the person therefore they are applicable to any size, any type or any industry that your company is in, and even to your private life as well!

Coaching is another tool that has been developing over the last couple of decades and that is unfortunately still highly misunderstood, miss-applied, but that has so much potential, so much power to help individuals work more efficiently in the workplace. Coaching is not only a set of techniques, it is an attitude and it is a mindset that can grow into a culture; the culture of asking questions. When was the last time your boss questioned you on an issue (usually negative)? How was your experience then? And with maybe another supervisor with a more directive style, who was just telling you what to do, how different was your motivation level after the instructions were given? How powerful were you feeling? How more accountable and in control were you feeling? Coaching is not about asking questions about your performance, about the past, but asking questions about the future, about what and how you can improve from now, about what solutions you can come up with, questions about how you can do things differently, better, faster. Have you ever had this kind of questions asked to you? I hope you have. If asked in an ineffective manner, your ego will potentially feel offended and have a knee-jerk reaction, thinking that the job that you have already done has been belittled or disregarded. If you have managed to shut your ego down for a while and look at opportunities for growth and if you have had the chance to be asked very potent questions, questions that make you pause for a second because you had never considered that perspective, because you had never dared to ask yourself this question, questions that people never asked you before, about your opinion, questions that made you ponder about other alternatives… how different was that interaction? Did you feel validated, respected, did you feel valued for bringing your own answers to the questions and your own solutions to the problems? How motivated were you feeling to act on these? How clear was the air before you? How much opportunity were you feeling available in front of you? This is the power of questions that is unfortunately underutilized. Coaching is the tool that uses questions as the main medium for achievement.

There are countless books on coaching that I would recommend and I would say that, if these tools presented here are the cogs, then coaching is a wonderful addition that is somehow like the grease that makes the whole mechanism work smoothly.

So go ahead and implement these tools, apply what you have discovered and what you have learned, have fun and enjoy. Learn even more, grow and develop, come back to the book to learn again, reach out to your full potential and achieve your goals. If you have any questions I would love to hear from you and I would love to discuss some of your goals, or if you simply want to send any feedback about this book, please contact me directly through LinkedIn, Twitter, or via email: xavierhalbi@gmail.com

Finally... not yet

Our journey on the mountain is not over. Although our goal is clear, as we go along our desires change so we adapt, we change our minds and we change ourselves. We grow. So we continue to walk our path, and now, with so much more clarity, flexibility, awareness, control and mastery we walk in a different way. We are more attentive to where we are going, we pay more attention to the steps that we make. We enjoy our surrounding, we discover the world around us, and re-discover ourselves. The journey does not end, we make it more enjoyable. We now understand that the path we walk is the path that we create for ourselves because it is about what the journey makes us become. The mountain is no more an obstacle to conquer, the mountain is our home, it is us and we are part of it. Now there is no more sense of hesitation. There is only a sense of enjoyment, curiosity, discovery and adventure.

Stay centered, keep learning, keep growing... and have fun!
- Xavier.

APPENDIX

VAK Test	Pg #145
List of Needs	Pg #152
List of Values	Pg #154
Skills self-assessment	Pg #160
The 7 Steps to an effective Personal Strategy	Pg #165
Suggested reading	Pg #172
Reference list	Pg #174

VAK Test

This test is for you to identify what importance your brain attaches to each of the 3 main senses:
- Visual
- Auditory
- Kinesthetic

Each question addresses situations in everyday life. For each question, give a score to each of the 3 answers of:

4 points, if this happens most often
2 points, if this happens from time to time
0 point, if this happens the least often

At the end of the test, total the scores for each A's, B's and C's, and plot them in the bottom graph.

1-What is the first thing that you remember when you took this book?
A)What you saw; the cover, the color, the quality of the cover
B)Something you heard when you took it, what you told yourself
C)The texture of the book, the weight of it, the feeling of the pages

2-What do you remember first about your last vacation (or weekend)?
A)What you saw, the place, the time of the day
B)What you heard, the people with you talking

C)What you did, how it felt

3-When you look for directions, you tend to:
A)Look at a map, GPS, smart phone
B)Ask a person on the way
C)Trust your guts, just continue… you'll get there

4-When you think about an object you like most, you like most about it:
A)The way it looks
B)The sounds about it, you hear yourself talk about it
C)The way it feels or the way it makes you feel

5-When you learn something new, you prefer to:
A)Watch the teacher, watch a video about it, read about it
B)Talk about what needs to be done
C)Jump in and practice yourself by copying the teacher

6-What do you recall more easily?
A)Faces
B)Names
C)How you felt or what you did with the person

7-What do you tend to say often?
A)Have a look, you look good
B)Listen, did you hear that? Sounds good
C)Cool, how are you feeling? Go for it, just do it

8-When you meet someone close you have not met for some time, you tend to:
A)Say: I'm so glad to see you!
B)Say: so nice to hear from you!
C)Go for a handshake or a hug

9-When you cook something new, you prefer to:

A) Read a recipe, watch a video about it
B) Listen to verbal instructions, although in a video, you listen to the person talk
C) Just follow your instincts, try it as you do

10- When demonstrating understanding to a person, you tend to say:
A) I see what you mean
B) I hear you
C) I know how you feel

11- When teaching someone, you generally tend to say:
A) Watch me do
B) Listen to what I am saying
C) Try it, you will figure it out

12- When you teach someone, you tend to:
A) Write instructions, draw
B) Explain verbally
C) Demonstrate and then let them try

13- When you build something like an Ikea furniture, you tend to;
A) Read the instructions first
B) Youtube a tutorial and listen attentively to the explanation
C) Just try it… cannot be that hard!

14- When you want to buy something new, say a phone, you tend to:
A) Look at the specifications
B) Talk about the product with the sales person
C) Manipulate it, touch it, feel it

15- When you shop for clothes, you tend to check first:
A) How it looks, the shape, the colors

B) Ask the sales person for assistance before finding anything
C) Check how the material feels, then when you try you check how it feels on you

16- You prefer people to communicate with you through:
A) Emails
B) Telephone
C) Face to face meeting

17- What do you remember first about your favorite band:
A) The jacket of the CD of your favorite album
B) A song that starts to play in your head
C) A feeling first, then the name or sound comes up

18- When rehearsing before a test, you tend to prefer:
A) Writing down notes & cheat sheets
B) Talk to yourself about the possible questions
C) Walk around the room, imagine doing the test

19- You tend to identify the words you hear as:
A) Images
B) Sounds
C) Feelings

20- During your free time, you prefer to:
A) Go to the cinema, an art gallery, watch a movie
B) Talk with friends, listen to music
C) Do some sports, do some manual work

21- Your hobbies are more likely to be:
A) Movies, books, photography
B) Music, talking with friends
C) A physical activity, playing an instrument, draw

22-When you want to keep in touch with a person you care and who is at the hospital
A)You write a card
B)You call
C)You visit them

23-At school you prefer(red)
A)Diagrams, charts, pictures & visual presentations
B)Discussions and lectures
C)Experiments and activities

24-When you have some time to spare, you prefer to:
A)Watch people go by
B)Listen to what they say, chat
C)Go for a stroll

25-When listening to see a concert, live or on TV, you prefer to:
A)Watch the show
B)Listen to the song and the lyrics
C)Start dancing or follow the beat and rhythm

26-You tend to hook around with people who:
A)Look and dress like you
B)Talk about the same topics
C)Do the same things

27-You are more often convinced by:
A)The body language of the person and how she looks
B)The tone of the voice of the person
C)If what is said feels right to you

28-When you agree with someone, you tend to say:
A)It looks right
B)It sounds right

C) It feels right

29- If you were at school, you would tend to prefer:
A) Arts
B) Philosophy
C) Sports or science

30- It is most easy for you to recognize:
A) See what is correct
B) Hear what sounds right
C) Feel what is right

31- Before going on vacation to a new destination, you prefer to:
A) Read about the place, read reviews online
B) Ask others what their experience there was
C) Imagine yourself there, or you just go

32- You prefer to relax by:
A) Watching a movie
B) Listening to some music
C) Taking a bath, rest on a very comfortable sofa

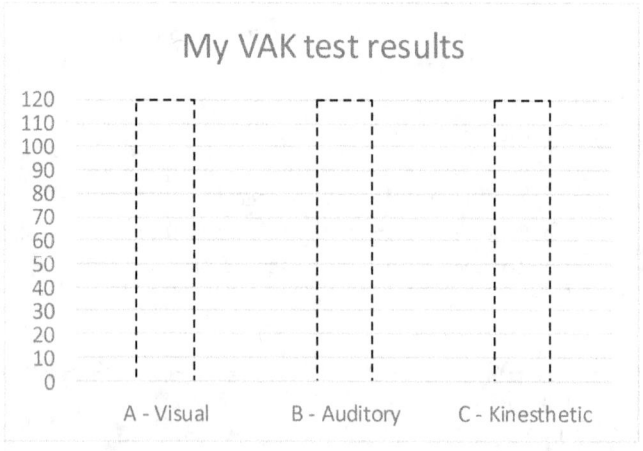

This chart represents the sense perceptions in order of preference of use.

Your highest score represents the sense that you tend to use more often and more easily to remember information. You also learn better and retain information much better if the information is received through this sense.

Your lowest score represents the sense that tends to be out of your conscious perception. This means that you will more likely be highly sensitive when receiving information through that sense.

A person with a very low score in Visual will be easily annoyed or irritated with certain color tones, or a certain level of brightness, if something does not "look" good, if someone is not dressed or shaved properly.

A person with a very low score in Auditory will be easily annoyed with *scritching* voice, with loud sounds, with beeping or *vrombing* sounds.

A person with a very low score in Kinesthetic will be easily annoyed with materials, fabrics, furniture that do not feel comfortable and with temperatures that are either too high or too low.

If your scores are relatively equal and balanced, then you are more flexible in the use of your senses. You will learn faster, retain information and remember things by using either of the senses. However, you might be irritated and irritable with certain things that are quite difficult for you to identify as they might be tapping into either of the 3 sense. It is important for you to identify the patterns of your triggers for irritation, maybe through journaling the situations that annoy you the most.

List of Needs

Approved
Abundance
Acclaimed
Accuracy
Achieve
Adored
Advise
Advocated
Affect others
Agreement
Alert
Allowed
Assurance
Attain
Attended to
Authority
Autonomous
Balance
Be a critical link
Be craved
Be devoted
Be heard
Be important
Be informed
Be known for
Be listened to
Be material
Be noticed
Be obeyed
Be obligated
Be remembered

Be useful
Busy-ness
Calmness
Candor
Capacity
Cared about
Career
Cautious
Celebrated
Checklists
Cherished
Clarity
Command
Comment
Commitments
Complimented
Confirmed
Consistency
Consummate
Cool
Correct
Correct others
Deferred to
Deliberate
Desired
Determination
Directness
Do the right thing
Dominate
Embraced
Encouraged

Esteemed
Exactness
Excess
Flattered
Follow
Forthrightness
Frankness
Fulfill
Fully informed
Get attention
Give
Given credit
Given gifts
Guarantees
Guarded
Have a cause
Have a task
Heeded
Held fondly
Helped
Honest
Honored
Immune
Improve others
Included
Independent
Indulgence
Industriousness
Influence
Initiative
Keep status quo

Liberated
Liked
Literalness
Loyalty
Luxury
Make a point
Manage
Might
Morally right
Non-scheming
Not be ignored
Not mistaken
Not obligated
Not work
Obey
Obviousness
Omnipotence
Opulence
Perfection
Performance
Permitted
Please others
Popular
Praised
Precision
Preferred
Prerogative
Privileged
Prized
Profit
Promises
Prosperity
Protected
Prove self
Quietness

Reach
Realize
Reconciliation
Regulated
Relished
Respected
Respite
Responsibility
Restrain
Restrict
Results
Rightness
Sanctioned
Satisfy others
Saved
Secure
Seen
Self-reliant
Sequentiality
Served
Share
Sincerity
Sovereign
Stable
Stamina
Steadiness
Stillness
Strength
Symmetry
Taken care of
Talk
Tasks
Tell stories
Thanked
Tolerated

Touched
Treasured
Treated tenderly
Trustfulness
Understood
Unity
Unrestricted
Unvarying
Valued
Vigilant
Vocation
Well regarded
Win
Worthy
Yield

CATEGORIES
BE ACCEPTED
BE ACKNOWL'D
BE RIGHT
TO ACCOMPLISH
BE LOVED
BE CARED FOR
CERTAINTY
TO CONTROL
BE FREE
BE COMFORTABLE
BE NEEDED
HONESTY
TO COMMUNICATE
DUTY
ORDER
PEACE
RECOGNITION
WORK
POWER
SAFETY

List of Values

Abundance
Acceptance
Accessibility
Accomplishm't
Accountability
Accuracy
Achievement
Acknowledg't
Acquire
Activeness
Adaptability
Adoration
Adroitness
Advancement
Adventure
Affection
Affluence
Aggressiveness
Agility
Alert
Alertness
Altruism
Amazement
Ambition
Amusement
Anticipation
Appreciation
Approachable
Approval
Arouse
Art

Articulacy
Artistry
Assemble
Assertiveness
Assist
Assurance
Attain
Attentiveness
Attract
Attractiveness
Audacity
Augment
Availability
Awareness
Awe
Balance
Be accepting
Be adept
Be amused
Be awake
Be aware
Be bonded
Be connected
Be devoted
Be entertained
Be exhilarated
Be expert
Be holy
Be honoring
Be imaginative
Be integrated

Be linked
Be original
Be part
of community
Be part
of family
Be passionate
Be present
Be religious
Be sensitive
Be spiritual
Be superior
Be the best
Be the greatest
Be with
Beauty
Being the best
Belonging
Benevolence
Bliss
Boldness
Bravery
Brilliance
Build
Buoyancy
Calmness
Camaraderie
Candor
Capability
Care
Carefulness

STRATEGIC FOOTSTEPS

- Catalyze
- Cause
- Celebrity
- Certainty
- Challenge
- Change
- Charity
- Charm
- Chastity
- Cheerfulness
- Clarity
- Cleanliness
- Clear-mindedness
- Cleverness
- Closeness
- Coach
- Comfort
- Commitment
- Community
- Compassion
- Competence
- Competition
- Completion
- Composure
- Conceive
- Concentration
- Confidence
- Conformity
- Congruency
- Connection
- Consciousness
- Conservation
- Consistency
- Contentment
- Continuity
- Contribute
- Contribution
- Control
- Conviction
- Conviviality
- Coolness
- Cooperation
- Cordiality
- Correctness
- Country
- Courage
- Courtesy
- Craftiness
- Create
- Create beauty
- Creativity
- Credibility
- Cunning
- Curiosity
- Danger
- Dare
- Daring
- Decisiveness
- Decorum
- Deference
- Delight
- Dependability
- Depth
- Design
- Desire
- Detect
- Determination
- Devotion
- Devoutness
- Dexterity
- Dignity
- Diligence
- Direction
- Directness
- Discern
- Discipline
- Discover
- Discovery
- Discretion
- Distinguish
- Diversity
- Dominance
- Dominate field
- Dreaming
- Drive
- Duty
- Dynamism
- Eagerness
- Ease
- Economy
- Ecstasy
- Edify
- Educate
- Education
- Effectiveness
- Efficiency
- Elation
- Elegance
- Embody
- elegance
- Embody excellence
- Embody grace
- Embody mastery
- Emote
- Empathize
- Empathy
- Encourage
- Encouragem't
- Endeavor
- Endow
- Endurance
- Energize
- Energy
- Enjoy sports
- Enjoyment
- Enlighten
- Enroll

- Entertainment
- Enthusiasm
- Environmentalism
- Ethics
- Euphoria
- Excellence
- Excitement
- Exhilaration
- Expectancy
- Expediency
- Experience
- Experience bliss
- Experience energy flow
- Experience gloriousness
- Experience hedonism
- Experience magnificence
- Experience sensuality
- Experience sex
- Experiment
- Expertise
- Explain
- Exploration
- Express refinement
- Express tenderness
- Expressiveness
- Extravagance
- Extroversion
- Exuberance
- Exude radiance
- Facilitate
- Fairness
- Faith
- Fame
- Family
- Fascination
- Fashion
- Fearlessness
- Feel
- Feel good
- Ferocity
- Fidelity
- Fierceness
- Financial independence
- Firmness
- Fitness
- Flexibility
- Flow
- Fluency
- Focus
- Fortitude
- Foster
- Frankness
- Freedom
- Friendliness
- Friendship
- Frugality
- Fun
- Gallantry
- Gamble
- Generosity
- Gentility
- Give pleasure
- Giving
- Glow
- Govern
- Grace
- Grant
- Gratitude
- Gregariousness
- Growth
- Guidance
- Guide
- Happiness
- Harmony
- Have fun
- Have impact
- Have taste
- Health
- Heart
- Helpfulness
- Heroism
- Hold preeminence
- Hold primacy
- Holiness
- Honesty
- Honor
- Hopefulness
- Hospitality
- Humility
- Humor
- Hygiene
- Imagination
- Impact
- Impartiality
- Improve
- Independence
- Individuality
- Industry
- Influence
- Influence
- Inform
- Ingenuity
- Inquisitiveness
- Insightfulness
- Inspiration
- Inspire
- Instruct
- Integrity
- Intellect

STRATEGIC FOOTSTEPS

- Intelligence
- Intensity
- Intimacy
- Intrepidness
- Introspection
- Introversion
- Intuition
- Intuitiveness
- Invent
- Inventiveness
- Investing
- Involvement
- Joy
- Judiciousness
- Justice
- Keenness
- Kindness
- Knowledge
- Lead
- Leadership
- Learn
- Learning
- Liberation
- Liberty
- Lightness
- Liveliness
- Locate
- Logic
- Longevity
- Love
- Loyalty
- Majesty
- Making a difference
- Marriage
- Mastery
- Maturity
- Meaning
- Meekness
- Mellowness
- Meticulousness
- Mindfulness
- Minister to
- Model
- Modesty
- Motivation
- Move forward
- Mysteriousness
- Nature
- Neatness
- Nerve
- Non-conformity
- Nurture
- Obedience
- Observe
- Open-mindedness
- Openness
- Optimism
- Order
- Organization
- Originality
- Outdo
- Outdoors
- Outlandishness
- Outrageous
- Partnership
- Passion
- Patience
- Peace
- Perceive
- Perceptiveness
- Perfect
- Perfection
- Perkiness
- Perseverance
- Persistence
- Persuade
- Persuasiveness
- Philanthropy
- Piety
- Plan
- Play games
- Playfulness
- Pleasantness
- Pleasure
- Poise
- Polish
- Popularity
- Potency
- Power
- Practicality
- Pragmatism
- Precision
- Predominate
- Prepare
- Preparedness
- Presence
- Prevail
- Pride
- Prime
- Privacy
- Proactivity
- Professionalism
- Prosperity
- Provide
- Prudence
- Punctuality
- Purity
- Quest
- Rationality
- Realism
- Realize
- Reason
- Reasonableness
- Recognition
- Recreation
- Refinement
- Reflection

- Reign
- Relate
- Relate with God
- Relaxation
- Reliability
- Relief
- Religiousness
- Reputation
- Resilience
- Resolution
- Resolve
- Resourceful
- Respect
- Respond
- Responsibility
- Rest
- Restraint
- Reverence
- Richness
- Rigor
- Risk
- Rule
- Sacredness
- Sacrifice
- Sagacity
- Saintliness
- Sanguinity
- Satisfaction
- Science
- Score
- Security
- See
- Self-control
- Selflessness
- Self-reliance
- Self-respect
- Sense
- Sensitivity
- Sensuality
- Serenity
- Serve
- Service
- Set standards
- Sexiness
- Sexuality
- Sharing
- Show compassion
- Shrewdness
- Significance
- Silence
- Silliness
- Simplicity
- Sincerity
- Skillfulness
- Solidarity
- Solitude
- Sophistication
- Soundness
- Spark
- Speculation
- Speed
- Spirit
- Spirituality
- Spontaneity
- Spunk
- Stability
- Status
- Stealth
- Stillness
- Stimulate
- Strength
- Strengthen
- Structure
- Success
- Support
- Supremacy
- Surprise
- Sympathy
- Synergy
- Synthesize
- Teach
- Teaching
- Teamwork
- Temperance
- Thankfulness
- The unknown
- Thoroughness
- Thoughtfulness
- Thrift
- Thrill
- Tidiness
- Timeliness
- Touch
- To unite
- Traditionalism
- Tranquility
- Transcendence
- Triumph
- Trust
- Trustworthy
- Truth
- Turn on
- Uncover
- Understanding
- Unflappability
- Uniqueness
- Unity
- Unstick others
- Uplift
- Usefulness
- Utility
- Valor
- Variety
- Venture
- Victory
- Vigor
- Virtue
- Vision

STRATEGIC FOOTSTEPS

Vitality	Watchfulness	Wisdom
Vivacity	Wealth	Wittiness
Volunteering	Willingness	Wonder
Warm-heartedness	Win	Worthiness
	Win over	Youthfulness
Warmth	Winning	Zeal

Skills Self-Assessment

Skill Name	Level of competence									
	1	2	3	4	5	6	7	8	9	10
Ability to change										
Ability to Train Others on Tasks										
Accepting criticism										
Administrative Management										
Analyzing Work Flow and Processes										
Argumentation										
Assembling, Constructing or Building										
Assessing Performance										
Assuming Team Membership Roles										
Balancing Work and Life										
Big Picture vision										
Budgeting										
Building rapport										
Business to Business Marketing										
Business Writing										
Calming oneself										
Career Development										
Cash-Flow Analysis										
Coaching										
Code writing										
Collaborating										

STRATEGIC FOOTSTEPS

Skill										
Communication										
Competitive Analysis and Planning										
Conflict Resolution										
Consultative Selling										
Consumer Marketing										
Cost Accounting										
Counseling										
Creating a vision										
Creative Thinking, Brainstorming										
Critical Thinking										
Critical thinking (evaluate, sort, analyze and relate info)										
Decision-making (respond quickly & bridge analysis & action)										
Decisiveness										
Delegating										
Directing										
Editing or Copyediting										
E-mail Communication										
Emotional Intelligence										
Empathy										
Execution										
Expression (verbal)										
Expression (written)										
Facilitation										
Financial Analysis										
Fixing or Repairing										
Forecasting										
Gain confidence from team										
Giving Feedback										
Graphics Software										
Grit & Resilience										

Group Problem Solving									
Handling complaints									
Hiring									
HTML / XML									
Implementation									
Influencing									
Internal Consulting									
Interviewing									
Keeping Teams on Target									
Keyboarding / Typing									
Leading									
Leading a Team									
Listening									
Making people feel comfortable									
Managing a Diverse Work Force									
Managing Change									
Managing Expectations									
Managing for Innovation									
Managing Upward									
Market Research (perform or direct)									
Marketing – Direct									
Marketing – Electronic									
Marketing – Product									
Marketing – Tele(-)									
Motivating									
Negotiating									
Networking									
Operating Tools or Machinery									
Organization									
Overcoming objections									
P&L Analysis									

STRATEGIC FOOTSTEPS

Persuasion										
Positivity										
Preparing a Business Plan										
Preparing an Investment Initiative										
Presentation										
Presentation Software										
Prioritization										
Problems Solving										
Project Management										
Promotions										
Proofreading										
Proposal / Contract Writing										
Publicity										
Quantitative Analysis										
Resourcefulness										
Responsibility (take)										
Running a Meeting										
Sales – Direct										
Sales – Tele(-)										
Seeing Multiple Perspectives										
Self-Awareness										
Self-control										
Self-monitoring										
Setting Goals and Objectives										
Speed reading										
Spreadsheet										
Strategic Planning										
Strategic Thinking										
Stress Management										
Tactical Planning										
Talent Retention										
Telesales										

Skill										
Time Management										
Tracking and Management										
Trade Show/Exhibits Management										
Training and Support Development										
Trend Analysis / Trend recognition										
Using Power and Authority Positively										
Vendor Management										
Working with a Virtual Team										
Writing										
Writing Policies										
Others:										

The 7 Steps to an effective Personal Strategy

Step 1 – What is my goal?

Criteria *Sample questions to answer*	**Description** of the goal by section
S – Specific *What do I really want to achieve? (stated in the positive)* *What are the specifics and rough details of this goal?*	
M – Measurable *How will I know when I have reached my goal?* *What will let me know that "this is it"?*	
A – Accountable *Do I believe that this is up to me to* *make it happen?* *Do I own it?* *Do I make my team responsible for achieving it? (for a goal imposed on someone else)*	
R – Relevant/Realistic *Is it aligned with your outcome?* *Is this goal realistically achievable, even if it means putting a lot of efforts, energy or attention to it?*	

T – Trackable *What is my deadline to reach this goal?* *What is the timeline of the milestones I give myself to reach this goal?*	
E – Environment *What might happen when the goal is reached?* *Who else will be affected during the process <u>and</u> once it is achieved?*	
R – Resources *Do I have the tools, material, skills or knowledge to achieve this goal?* *Does the team/person have the tools, power or means to reach this goal?*	

S – Senses/Sensory *Describe what you see, what you hear, what you smell, with as much detail as you can, of the entire situation & surrounding*	
T – Touch *Describe how you feel inside, now that you have achieved this goal. Where is the feeling? What shape, color, sound?*	

Criteria *Sample questions to answer*	**Description** of my goal - by section
M – My goal *Whose goal is this?* *Who had the idea of achieving this goal?*	
I – Inspired/Insight/ Intuition *Did this goal come as a thought process or as an insight, an intuition?* *If it was a thought process, check it through your intuition. How does it feel to imagine you already achieved it?* *Do I feel inspired to reach this goal?*	
N – New *Is this a new goal, one that I have not heard about?* *How is it different from other goals?* *What makes this goal different and special?*	
E – Excitement/ Energized *How do I feel about the prospect of achieving this goal?* *How excited am I about adventuring on the path to reaching this goal?*	

My SMARTER, SMARTEST goal which is also MINE, in one sentence:

_____
_____
_____
_____
_____
_____

Step 2 – Where am I?
My VAK:

_____

Reader / Listener:

_____

My top 5 Needs:

_____
_____
_____
_____
_____

My top 5 Values:

_____
_____
_____
_____
_____

My Center:

_____

Step 3 – Road Map
How will I get there?

_____

_____

Step 4 – Tools
My top 5 skills:

_____

_____

_____

_____

_____

How do I learn best?

_____

My Strengths & Weaknesses

My Strengths	My Weaknesses

My habits:

_____

_____

My motivation: External or Internal reference:

_____

Step 5 – Make the first step
How do I operate?

	Avoider	Wanter
Thinker	1 Procrastinator	2 Yes but
Doer	3 Start-Stop	4 Go for it

What is the next thing to do?
_____

Who will take action on that?
_____

When?
_____

Step 6 – Forget the goal
How do I prefer to clear my mind?
_____

How do I relax best?
_____

When is the best time for me to relax?
_____

Where?
_____

Step 7 – Enjoyment
What stresses me?

What bores me?

What excites me?

What conditions are needed for me to be "in the flow"?

Do I need more challenges or more skills to face my current situation?

Where can I get them from?

Suggested reading

7 habits of highly effective people – Steven Covey, 1989

Coaching for performance – John Whitmore, 1992

Co-active coaching – Kimsey-House, Sandahl, Whitworth, 2007

Crucial conversations – Patterson, Grenny, McMillan, Swatzler, 2002

Difficult personalities – Helen McGrath & Hazel Edwards, 2000

Don't sweat the small stuff... and it's all small stuff – Richard Carlson, 1997

Feel the fear and do it anyway – Susan Jeffers, 1987

Flow, the psychology of optimal experience – Mihaly Csikszentmihalyi, 1990

Genius – James Bannerman, 2012

How the mind works – Steven Pinker, 1997

How to disagree without being disagreeable – Suzette Haden Elgin, 1997

How to get from where you are to where you want to be – Jack Canfield, 2005

How to get what you want without having to ask – Richard Templar, 2011

How to manage your mammoth – Wendy Jago, 2012

How to raise your self-esteem – Nathaniel Branden, 1987

How to stop worrying and start living – Dale Carnegie, 1953

How to talk to anyone – Leil Lowndes, 1999

How to win friends and influence people – Dale Carnegie, 2004

I'm ok, you're ok – Thomas A. Harris, 1973

Masterful coaching – Robert Hargrove, 2008

NLP, the new technology of achievement – Steve Andreas & Charles Faulkner, 1996

Secrets of the people whisperer – Perry Wood, 2004

Supercoach – Michael Neill, 2009
The chimp paradox – Steve Peters, 2012
The magic of rapport – Jerry Richardson, 2000
The new people making – Virginia Satir, 1988
The power of habit – Charles Duhigg, 2012
Using your brain for a change – Richard Bandler, 1985
Working with emotional intelligence – Daniel Goleman, 1998
Words that change minds – Shelle Rose Charvet, 1995

Reference list

Eduard DeBono – Simplicity, 1998 – Penguin Life
John Spence – Awesomely Simple, 2009 – Wiley
David Swartz – The Magic of Thinking Big, 1995 – Pocket Books
Andy Waroll – Marilyn Monroe, 1962
Napoleon Hill – Think & Grow Rich, 1937 – TarcherPerigee
Edward DeBono – Lateral Thinking, 2014 – Vermilion
Edward DeBono – Serious Creativity, 1993 – Harperbusiness
Synchronicity: The Inner Path of Leadership – J. Jaworsky & P. Senge, 2011 – Berrett-Koehler Publishers
Jim Rohn: Creating your vision for the future – www.jimrohn.successacademy.com
He who knows others is wise. He who knows himself is enlightened – Lao Zi, 6th-5th century – China
What brought you here will not get you there – M. Goldsmith, 2007 – Hachette Books
You cannot solve a problem with the same mind that created it – Einstein, 1879-1955
Johari window is a technique, a tool that is great to understand what is going on in your communication created by Joseph Luft (1916-2014) and Harrington Ingham (1916-1995) in 1955
Tony Robbins says that there are two pains: the pain of discipline and the pain of regret – https://www.tonyrobbins.com
NLP, Neuro-Linguistic Programing, a behavioral change and personal improvement technology with therapeutic effects was developed in the 70's by Richard Bandler and John Grinder
Stephen Covey – Principle Centered Leadership, 1992 – Fireside Press
Stephen Hawking – On the shoulder of giants, 2003 –

Running Press
NLP presuppositions –
https://anlp.org/presuppositions-of-nlp
Napoleon Hill – ibid.
Thomas J. Leonard – 28 laws of attraction, 2007 – Scribner
Dao De Jing, 6th-5th century – China, Lao Zi said:
He who understands others has wisdom
He who understands oneself has clarity of mind
Robin Sharma – The leader who had no title, 2010 – Free Press
Charles Duhigg – The power of habits, 2014 – Random House Trade Paperbacks
YouTube: Anthony Robbins – How To Develop Daily Rituals To Live Exceptional Life!!!
Edward DeBono – Six Thinking Hats, 1999 – Back Bay Books
A national survey was completed with 4,000 senior US executives
L. Bossidy & R. Charan – Execution, 2011 – Random House Business
Do the thing and you shall have power – Ralph Waldo Emerson
Shantideva a mystical teacher of Ancient Tibet said Why worry if it can be remedied? And why worry if it cannot be remedied?
Execution – ibid.
CNNInteractive–'StillMe'
http://edition.cnn.com/books/dialogue/9805/reeve/index.html?iref=newssearch
You need to be cautious when others are greedy, and be greedy when others are cautious – Waren Buffett
Mihaily Csikszentmihalyi – Flow, 2008 – Harper Perennial Modern Classics
Richard Carlson – Don't sweat the small stuff, 1997 – Hyperion

Bashar (Darryl Anka) www.bashar.org

Life is not measured by the number of breaths we take but by the number of moments that take our breath away – Not sure who
http://quoteinvestigator.com/2013/12/17/breaths/

John Spence – Ibid.

Peter Senge – The fifth discipline, 2006 – Doubleday

Robin Sharma – Ibid.

S. Covey – The 7 habits of highly effective people, 2013 – Simon & Schuster

Lolly Daskal – The Leadership Gap, 2017 – Portfolio

Virginia Satir – Your many faces, 2009 – Celestial Arts

Dr. Jon Kabat-Zinn – Coming to our senses, 2006 – Hachette Books

Niccolo Machiavelli – The Prince, 1992 – Dover Publications

"The Minute You Stop Chasing Trends Is When You Will Start Building a Real Business" – Kimanzi Constable
https://www.entrepreneur.com/article/300345?utm_source=newsletter&utm_medium=email

Simon Sinek – Start with why, 2011 – Portfolio

ABOUT THE AUTHOR

Xavier has 20+ years of experience in the service industry. He has a Cornell/IMHI MBA, he is a certified NLP Master Practitioner, Professional Coach, mentor and speaker. He specialized in Strategy, Organizational Behavior and Personal Development. He has helped 100's find their motivations, improve their careers and combine the two to make their lives more fulfilling.

www.ingramcontent.com/pod-product-compliance
Lightning Source LLC
Chambersburg PA
CBHW052315220526
45472CB00001B/125